Beautiful Moves

BEAUTIFUL MOVES

DESIGNING STADIA

Benjamin Flowers

First published in 2018 by Lund Humphries

Lund Humphries
Office 3, Book House
261A City Road
London EC1V 1JX
UK

www.lundhumphries.com

ISBN (hardback): 978–1–84822–224–3

A Cataloguing-in-Publication record for this book is
available from the British Library.

Front cover: New San Mames, Bilbao, Spain.
Photo: Aitor Ortiz.

Back cover: Borisov Arena, Barysaw, Belarus.
Photo: Tomaz Gregoric.

Copy edited by Julie Gunz
Designed by Jacqui Cornish
Set in Arnhem Pro and Founders Grotesk Text
Printed in China

Contents

Acknowledgements

In researching and writing this book I have benefited from the input and advice of many, who deserve thanks for their assistance. First, the group of dedicated students at the School of Architecture at Georgia Tech who were research assistants for this project, in particular: Ryan Adams, Reem Alshamaa, Michael Coffman, Andrew Colturi, Akintunde Erophillips, Yingfie Liu, Monica Rizik, Candace Seda, Amy Stone, Sara Yoo, Liu Yue and Lu Zhang. Second, the members of my research group, Stadia Lab: Gustavo do Amaral, Zachary Hicks, Charlotte Steinichen, Brian Castro and Elizabeth Sit. I was fortunate to have many thought-provoking conversations with Geraint John, Tom Jones, Mike Hall, Erleen Hatfield and other colleagues in firms working on stadia projects around the world, as well as with the members of the International Union of Architects' Sports and Leisure Working Programme. A Faculty Development Grant from the College of Design at Georgia Tech was crucial to the production of this book, for which I am grateful.

1   Introduction

The only way to deal with death is to transform everything that precedes it into art.

Arsene Wenger[1]

The past two decades have witnessed a revolution in global football. Much of this, most of it for many, has been about money. The sums attached to the game have exploded. The cost of tickets has skyrocketed. The transfer fees and wages for players are now eye-watering. Broadcast fees and revenues dwarf those of all other endeavours and viewership numbers run in the billions. For many, money, for better and often worse, is now the defining element of modern football.

There is, on the other hand, another story – one about beauty. These decades saw a profound burst of creative effort on the pitch. Two teams in particular defined a decade of beautiful play: Barcelona (Barca) and Arsenal (managed by Arsene Wenger). The beauty of Barca's play in the first two decades of the twenty-first century is undeniable – but also not entirely surprising. It was, after all, a grand club with a proud tradition of unique football. Nevertheless, many observers opined that the Barca of the first two decades of the twenty-first century was perhaps the most skilled, most inventive, and perhaps greatest team ever assembled. This is a subject that makes for a surefire argument-starter among fans and journalists alike around the world.

Arsenal, however, was a whole different story. Prior to the arrival of Arsene Wenger in 1996, Arsenal was famous for 'boring, boring' football. One-nil to the Arsenal may have pleased hardcore fans, but few others.[2] So, when Wenger arrived and over the next several years brought in Dennis Bergkamp, Thierry Henry, Robert Pires, Patrick Vieira and countless other players who played not just effectively, but attractively, he began a revolution in English football. Over the next decade a distinctive Arsenal style emerged, one described by adjectives that could just as easily apply to artistic endeavours – creative, dynamic, free flowing and so forth. Today, there are teams all over the world that aspire to play 'in the Arsenal way', a condition unimaginable 30 years ago.[3]

The architectural revolution

There was another revolution taking place in those years – one off the pitch but even more significant for this volume. The stadium, a building type that for decades, even centuries, had sat largely outside the purview of architectural judgement was, rather unexpectedly, catapulted into the upper tiers of architectural expression. The jinking, creative footballer on the pitch no longer played among straightforward stands or in a drab concrete bowl. Increasingly the beautiful moves on the field were performed in spaces of equivalent attractiveness. The money that poured into so many other aspects of the game was now reimagining and reinventing the space in which play took place. Parametric football of the sort Barca and Arsenal perfected could now be played in parametric stadia (see, for instance, the Aviva Stadium).

This development actually had its origins in the post-World War II era, but it was easy to miss it as the transformation was taking place. Likewise, there were outside forces pushing the evolution of the stadium from an engineering problem to a site of architectural exploration, many of which I will touch on later. Nevertheless, it is the case that today, in any given city around the world, it is likely that the single largest, most complex and most expensive structure in the built landscape is a stadium. In many cities it might be one of the only structures designed by a world-famous, even Pritzker Prize-winning architect (for the former think of the Peter Eisenman-designed University of Phoenix Stadium in 2006, for the latter Eduardo Souto de Moura's Estadio Municipal in the industrial city of Braga in Portugal). This volume charts the transformation of this building type, with a special focus on projects since the 1960s that propelled the architectural ambitions of the stadium forward.

Beauty as an organising criterion

There are a number of qualities that one could yoke a project such as this to: a focus on the scale of the stadium – its bigness, for instance – would produce a significant cohort of structures for analysis, from Pyongyang (the Rungrado 1st of May Stadium) to the small towns that are home to the Universities of Michigan and Penn State (Ann Arbor and State College respectively) to the capitals of Mexico and Brazil (Mexico City and Brasilia). If the filter was the relative fame and success of the club (either past or present), then one might end up with a list of stadia from Italy, Germany, Spain and England. If the criteria were cost, then the list would tilt decidedly towards the recent past, with projects

such as the Mercedes-Benz Stadium in Atlanta ($1.6 billion), New Wembley ($1.4 billion) and the proposed stadium for Los Angeles ($2.6 billion). Here, however, I am interested in a different organising criterion – beauty.

Beauty is a challenging value to deploy as an organising framework for a variety of reasons, but these also represent the very virtues of beauty as an organising ideal. First, beauty depends on context, or in an architectural sense, site. Many of the projects featured in this volume gain some degree of their expressive power from their relationship to or ingenious exploitation of their physical location (the Borisov Arena by OFIS Architects, for instance, or the SESC Pompeia by Lina Bo Bardi). Second, beauty can be generated by novel material uses, as in the polycarbonate tiles of the Aviva Stadium by Populous, or the weave-like concrete of Beijing Olympic Stadium by Herzog and de Meuron. Finally, beauty can emerge when light and form interact in striking ways, as is the case with many of the projects pictured here.

The notion of beauty as a quality associated with stadia is a complicated one for many reasons. Stadia are generally regarded by the general public as utilitarian structures, designed (or engineered) to allow for activities to take place and for observation thereof. Architects often, both past and present, treat the stadium as a pragmatic structure, a problem to be solved, within budget and on time. Though the scale is as grand as many cathedrals, rarely has any architect or architectural historian waxed eloquent on the procession through a stadium, and rarer less have those same commented on the significance of the stadium relative to the life and culture of a place. In the second decade of the twenty-first century stadia are often the most expensive, most technologically complex, and most hotly debated projects of any city around the world. And yet, though politicians and the general public may be brought to heated exchange when discussing these buildings, rarely does the architectural discourse around them match that level of energy.

This is so for a number of reasons, some reasonable and others less so. For most of the history of the stadium, from the Coliseum in Rome to the great arenas in France or the stadia of Greece to Old Trafford in Manchester or New Yankee Stadium in the Bronx, the goal has been the production of awe and the sublime. Scale and spectacle rather than the detail and the pursuit of beauty ruled the day. Certainly, all of these projects have architectural qualities that are admired. But they are impressive for reasons quite distinct from beauty in the way architects and critics celebrate other building types. Stadia designers pursued impressiveness, and to that extent a certain mode of architectural expression did emerge, but impressiveness does not demand or require beauty. And that is why, in large part, visitors to the modern secular cathedrals just mentioned certainly remember their experience there. But they do so largely for reasons unrelated to architectural aesthetics.

That is what makes the shift towards architecturally ambitious stadia especially significant for this volume but also for cities and societies as well. The move to pursuing beauty is not without cost. Many of the buildings in the following pages are not merely objects in space, indeed they are expected to be agents for change in the surrounding urban landscape. There are upsides and, unfortunately, downsides to this situation. Beauty is not expensive per se, but complexity and programmatic heft often are. And so, the layering of obligations onto stadia over the past decades has driven up the cost of stadia construction and operation considerably. In flush times, politicians and voters are often content to bear the costs of beauty and ambition. When leaner times arrive, as they inevitably do, perspectives change, making stadia particularly vulnerable to slipping from admired addition to the cityscape to widely criticised white elephant (see, for example, the Olympic grounds of Athens from the 2004 Summer Games).

Stadia as targets

It is important to keep in mind the range of political, economic and cultural factors that are layered onto stadia, both the beautiful ones and those less so. The meanings attached to these buildings are not fixed. They change over time and so too must our interpretations of their architectural significance. There is in addition an utterly depressing turn of events that has emerged in the last decade that any observer or critic of stadia must confront: stadia as targets for terrorism and political violence. Politics, of course, have been a part of the long history of great public buildings, and stadia are no different. There are myriad examples in history of moments when politics made their way into stadia, whether in the form of riots or abandoned matches, or stadia deployed for a range of non-sporting ends (prisons, refugee camps and the like).[4] But there is something distinct about the present condition, where stadia are not only spaces for intermixing politics and sport, but rather targets of political violence in and of themselves.

What this means is that, in many parts of the world, stadia are carrying multiple heavy loads. On the one hand, they are designed to be places of spectacle, of entertainment, of an inward focus away from the outside world and directed instead to the play on the ground. On the other, they are also now designed to increasingly unyielding standards designed to minimise the threat of violent attack. Both sets of manoeuvres must take place in the same space, at the same time, without the one ever compromising the success of the other. Many of the measures put in place for security are apparent and familiar from other venues, such as metal detectors or CCTV. Others are equally obvious, but only to the trained eye. The National Football League, for instance, obligates all stadia used in the league to have minimum setbacks from adjacent roadways in order to protect from vehicle bomb blasts. But to most passersby, the setbacks are no more than landscape choices, not markers of the fear of targeted political violence. And so, as stadia projects rise again and again around the world, often to ever-grander heights of formal achievement and technological complexity, they do so now in an age of risk.

Football without stadia

A game of football does not demand a stadium. Indeed, a football pitch can appear almost anywhere, under almost any condition, a reality beautifully documented by Neville Gabie in his wonderful book *Posts*. In it, Gabie photographs the provisional goalposts found around the world to enable the game of football to be played. As Gabie writes, 'no matter where in the world, goalposts are so familiar a part of the landscape they go unnoticed. They exist like street lights or telegraph poles, necessary but unconsidered.'[5] Some of the most interesting pitches are found far from a grand stadium – scruffy places where the passion for the game makes up for the absence of concessions, covered stands, stands at all, or sometimes even grass. One could write a volume on these spaces and how they organise the life of the communities in which they sit. But this is not our concern here. Instead, we are here to find the exceptional.

1a

1b

1c

(from top)
1a. Belfast, Northern Ireland, LAT 54.62085 LONG -5.921483; 1b. Carasebes, Romania, LAT 45.418541 LONG 22.217657; 1c. Conelia, Free State Province, South Africa, LAT -27.339267 LONG 25.090767; 1d. Halley Research Centre, Antarctica, LAT -75.6046300 LONG -26.2090000; 1e. Liverpool, England, LAT 53.398088 LONG -2.932148; 1f. Liverpool, England, LAT 53.4268 LONG -2.996883; 1g. Punta Arenas, Chile, LAT -53.157585 LONG -70.88849; 1h. Punta Arenas, Chile, LAT -53.157585 LONG -70.88849.

1d

1e

1f

1g

1h

11

2 Riverfront Stadium, Cincinnati, Ohio, the rise of the 'cookie-cutter' concrete bowl.

2 1960: The Postwar Stadium and the City

The concrete bowl

For many, the 1960s represent the high point of the concrete bowl stadium. Whether looking at an American baseball field like the Riverfront Stadium in Cincinnati (Heery and Heery, 1970, demolished 2002) or the Maracana Stadium in Brazil (Ramos et al., 1950), the ubiquity of the concrete bowl is hard to understate. Although generally used as a term of derision and opprobrium today, there were nevertheless moments of beauty to be found among the stadia of the 1960s, even in the confines of the bowl.

Football was a different beast in the 1960s. Games were mostly seen in person – television broadcasts were much rarer, and seldom crossed national boundaries. There certainly were not the global marketing juggernauts of today to broadcast games and, perhaps just as importantly, pump billions of dollars into the sport. Boots came mostly in black, jerseys were free of advertising and pitches were lumpy when they weren't merely muddy. The game was perhaps purer in many ways, but it was also, to be honest, often uglier too.

Off the field, things were not much better. Stadia were generally pragmatic affairs and often, to put it charitably, in a state best described as 'deferred maintenance'. The issue wasn't just one of aesthetics – frequent disasters were a reminder that the working-class spirit of football came with its own costs, both philosophical and physical. The

focus of most stadia in this decade was to fit as many people into the stands as possible, with little or no variation in the cost of entry to the ground depending on where one planned to sit (or, more likely, stand). At many stadia in many countries, once you had your ticket stamped upon entry, you could move around in the stands to find a vantage point that suited you best. The only distraction from the action on the pitch might be a large clock or, even more rarely, an antiquated scoreboard. Bars, restaurants or even ample and well-appointed lavatory facilities were practically unheard of in these years. Stadia were mostly named after the neighbourhoods or streets where they were located or a local figure of note. Corporate purchases of naming rights were extremely rare – with exceptions coming, no surprise, in the United States in the form of, among others, Wrigley Field (Zachary Taylor Davis, 1914) and Busch Memorial Stadium (Sverdrup & Parcel, 1966). These were named after chewing gum and beer empires respectively, with the latter especially notable from a design perspective for its crowning, arched roof designed by Edward Durrell Stone. The arched roof was a specific reference to the city of St Louis and the Gateway Arch project by Eero Saarinen completed a year earlier.

Things did not change much on this front for the first few decades after World War II. I recall growing

3   Wrigley Field, Chicago, Illinos, opened in 1914 as Weeghman Park and was later renamed after the chewing gum magnate William Wrigley Jr and his eponymous corporation.

4   Busch Memorial Stadium, St Louis, Missouri, named after a family-owned beer empire and whose roofline references the iconic Gateway Arch in the background.

5   Fenway Park, Boston, Massachusetts, the 'Green Monster'.

up in football-mad Central America where I saw very few of the 1982 World Cup games on television, even though Honduras had qualified for the World Cup for the first time – mostly I listened to matches on the radio with the neighbours. Aside from the radio, sports were largely a pastime one played, saw at a stadium or read about in the paper. In this context, the public perception of the stadium tended to be about the game, with far less of an emphasis on the experience of the building apart from the sport it housed. In part because of this, the sense of the stadium as an architectural object was minimised. Notable design features, to the extent that they existed or were widely acknowledged by the public,

tended to focus on size or colour. Perhaps the best example of this combined both: the green 37-foot left field wall at Fenway Park in Boston (James McLaughlin, 1912). Called simply 'the wall' for most of its history, it is also today commonly referred to as 'the Green Monster'.

Structural innovation in the 1960s

Houston Astrodome

The conjoined forces of increased spectator security and regulation at matches and the explosive growth in the fees associated with broadcast rights radically reshaped the spaces in which football was played, in most ways for the better (although I will touch on this later). Even in the United States, where stadia were generally grander than many of their South American, United Kingdom and European counterparts, the level of design was mostly driven by engineering concerns rather than architectural ones. Aesthetics, to the extent they were discussed at all, were expected to be generated by scale, by greatness of size, rather than by other, more poetic sensibilities. Even still, there are some notable projects that bear mentioning. The Astrodome in Houston (Hermon Lloyd & W.B. Morgan, 1965) is perhaps the most famous American stadium of this era. Often called the 'eighth wonder of the world', the Astrodome was the first domed stadium in the world.[6] Though still standing at present, I use the past tense as it is no longer used as a sporting ground and is partially demolished. A multi-purpose venue, it was not especially beautiful in perspective or elevation from a distance, which is how, like most monumental buildings, it was often photographed. Up close though it did possess a number of refined features: a pleasing concrete screen wall with pre-cast concrete diamond forms set between rhythmically situated thin ribs wrapping around the facade, features that call to mind the decorative

modernism of Minoru Yamasaki. There were also thin concrete roofs at the various apertures that allowed for entry, reminiscent of Eero Saarinen's heterogeneous modernism, and finally muscularly realised cylinders housing ingress and egress staircases that echo the work of Louis Kahn.

On the interior the Astrodome had several striking features, the grandest of them the skylight ceiling. The scale of the roof structure alone was noteworthy. When illuminated by daylight, however, the impression on the interior generated by rectangular skylights set within the monumental triangles of the roof structure, set within the even larger triangular slices that curved down to meet the lip of the upper bowl, was a truly spectacular sight, unlike anything else in the world. This did have the unintended consequence of making it impossible for fielders to clearly see foul balls, which might at least have led to higher scoring games. Unfortunately for the Astrodome, it fell victim to the same fate that has befallen so many other, less visually impressive structures. It was declared 'obsolete' and its tenant teams moved out, leaving a former marvel of the world to crumble slowly into decline. An even more ignominious fate befell another grand project from that era, Shea Stadium (Praeger-Kavanagh-Waterbury, 1964). An open-air, multi-sport concrete bowl, Shea was not precisely

6   Houston Astrodome, Texas, showing the surprisingly delicate pre-cast concrete screens.

8   Houston Astrodome, the diamond shapes in the translucent roof echoing those on the facade.

beautiful, but it was monumental. In 2008 it was demolished to make way for a parking lot. Stadia, for all their monumentality and cost, are often among the shortest-lived buildings in American cities (their longevity tends to be greater in other parts of the world).

Ingalls Hockey Rink

Other novel stadium projects in the United States from this era include Saarinen's Ingalls Hockey Rink at Yale University (1958) with its elegant double-curve roof that hangs from a central arched concrete backbone. On the interior, the clear expression of the site-cast concrete rib and the timber roof hanging from the cable system offers both an explanation of how the building is put together as well as a poetic quality that adds drama to the action taking place on the rink. At the time of its completion, the rink was on the edge of campus, and Saarinen saw his idiosyncratic and elegant design as a way to draw students and faculty to the building. Completed just three years before his death, Ingalls cemented Saarinen's reputation as an unorthodox modern architect willing to embrace a highly expressive architectural language.

Miami Marine Stadium

Ingalls is today a famous structure, taught to architecture students around the world, but a lesser-known project from that era also merits consideration: Miami Marine Stadium by Hilario Candela (1963). Candela was an architect who had recently arrived in Miami from Cuba when he received the commission for the stadium at the young age of 28. The programme is one that is distinctly American and distinctly Miami: a set of covered stands perched on the water's edge to allow spectators to watch speedboat races. Built entirely of site-cast concrete, the stadium was a popular venue for motorboat races and concerts, until damage from Hurricane Andrew in 1992 left it condemned by the city as unsafe for use. Candela's design, now graffiti-covered and in significant disrepair, still channels his original intent: to recall the structural elegance of Pier Luigi Nervi's Fiorentina

9   Houston Astrodome was a modern coliseum and at one time called the 'eighth wonder of the world'.

10   Ingalls Hockey Rink, New Haven, Connecticut, Eero Saarinen's elegant collegiate ice rink.

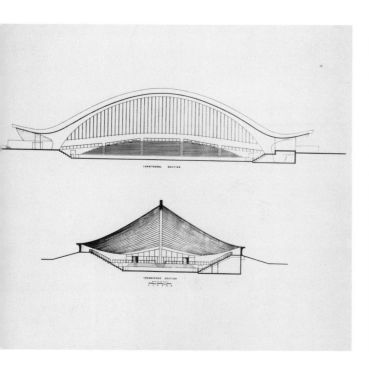

11   Ingalls Hockey Rink, showing how the beauty in the structure guides the quality of interior space.

12   Ingalls Hockey Rink, note how the curve of the retaining wall turns up into the roof.

13   Miami Marine Stadium, Florida, Hilario Candela's site-cast concrete stand for observing powerboat racing.

14   Fiorentina Stadium, Florence, Italy, a curved stair at Pier Luigi Nervi's 1931 project.

15   Fiorentina Stadium, showing the iconic cantilevered roof.

Stadium of 1931 and even a bit of the glamour of the 1941 Zarzuela Hippodrome in Madrid by Eduardo Torroja. The latter is undeniably crisper, rendered in Corbusian white rather than Candela's more *béton brut* affair, but then again, Miami is not Madrid, and thoroughbreds are prettier than motorboats.

Palazzetto dello Sport

Nervi was still active in these years, and he was the engineer (working with architect Annibale Vitellozzi) behind Rome's Palazzetto dello Sport, completed in 1957 for the 1960 Summer Olympic Games. Far more modest in scale than the Astrodome, it demonstrates a similar interest in how an articulated, thoughtful domed structure can be at once heavy on the outside and lightweight on the

inside. The arena is ringed on the exterior by a series of linked, inward-leaning 'Y' concrete members resembling human figures with their arms raised. These seem to hold up a thin shell of a concrete roof that resembles a seashell (or possibly a pie crust depending on your point of view). Glazing is tucked away several feet behind the exterior structure, and brick infill walls meet the ground plane. On the interior, much like the Astrodome, the show really kicks off.

Yoyogi National Gymnasium

Nervi's primary responsibility was designing the dome, and its intricate and elegant rib structure resembles lacework more than reinforced pre-cast concrete. Spanning 60 metres, it is both an

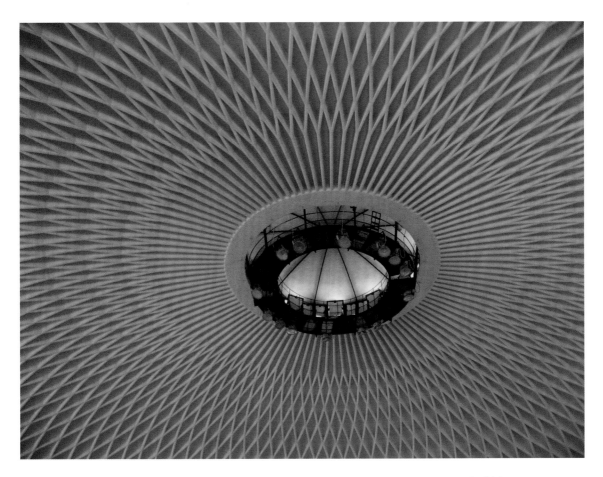

16　Palazzetto dello Sport, Rome, Italy, another of Nervi's fine sporting structures, this one a wonderful dome.

17   Yoyogi National Gymnasium, Tokyo, Kenzo
Tange's groundbreaking design and a symbol of a
new, modern Japan.

ingenious structural engineering solution and a powerfully realised celebration of the material capacities of concrete. It was among many Olympic projects in the 1960s that used concrete particularly effectively. Several years later Kenzo Tange pushed the envelope of concrete sporting architecture even further with his Yoyogi National Gymnasium for the 1964 Summer Olympic Games in Tokyo. Justifiably famous today for its iconic curves, it was at the time very much a groundbreaking undertaking. What was then the world's largest suspended roof span joins an extravagantly curved concrete base, and the whole takes on the form, depending on your point of view, of a seashell, a boat or a variation on a Japanese pagoda. Though relatively modest in scale, these were projects that sought to represent something heroic and modern, and spoke to the ambitions of both Italy and Japan to be seen in an international context as advanced nation-states with highly developed technical and building cultures. They were in many ways significantly more complex projects (aesthetically and structurally) than the array of so-called 'cookie-cutter' stadia that dominated much of the stadium landscape over the next several decades.

The legacy of the 1960s

The 1960s offered a mixed bag in terms of stadia. Although concrete bowl structures were the norm, at the other end of the spectrum Nervi and Tange were creating Olympic venues of tremendous sculptural grace and material rigour, projects that also succeeded in having a legacy function and are still prized by architects and the general public, something rare among Olympic venues.[7] Then you had the Astrodome with all of its advances – air conditioning, a 220-metre dome that sits nearly 18 storeys above the ground, the invention of AstroTurf to replace natural grass, and the world's first animated electronic scoreboard among them. But, of course, the Astrodome was also a multi-purpose stadium, one that presaged a whole generation of far less technologically or formally inventive heirs that would dot the landscapes of

cities around the world over the next two to three decades. And those stadia would increasingly come to define the face of sporting architecture, sometimes for the better, but mostly for the worst.

The 1960s were also years of remarkable creativity. As the second decade of the twenty-first century unfolds, a whole new generation of architects are rediscovering Candela's delightful Miami Marine Stadium and moves are finally underway to restore that wonderful project to a state appropriate to its contribution to the built culture of the city. There were even other ambitions for stadia in the 1960s that went unfulfilled, but which should be mentioned here. In the early 1960s the city of San Diego, seeing how much Houston had taken advantage of promoting the Astrodome as a lure to bring tourists to the city, proposed construction of a new stadium, one that would attract even more press and attention than the Astrodome. The owner of the American Football League team in San Diego at the time was Barron Hilton, heir to the hotel chain fortune. His team, and the local baseball team, played in a cramped, older ground called Balboa Stadium. Barron's father, Conrad, had long used the decidedly modern architecture of his hotels around the world as advertisements for the merits of capitalist democracy, and Barron was also sensitive to the uses of architecture for a variety of political and economic ends. He proposed that the new stadium – seating 50,000 and dubbed All-American Stadium – would float on Mission Bay. The floating stands could be reconfigured depending on the use on a given day. It would, Hilton claimed, 'be the first novel idea in stadium building since the dome'.[8]

An engineering firm was hired to generate speculative proposals, the city council was convinced to come on board with the plan, and press releases went out heralding the project. Shortly afterwards, an architecture firm was hired to generate preliminary design studies and to work out a more detailed budget for the project. And that was as far as it got. The architects revealed what most observers had thought all along: that such a project would surely cost twice as much as a conventional stadium, even if the city owned the property on which it was built. Efforts were made to improve

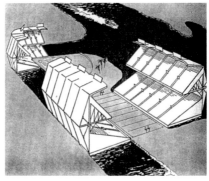

18   San Diego Floating Stadium proposal, a never-realised fantasy, pictured here in both baseball and American football modes.

the design, but in the end the plans were shelved, and a conventional, earth-bound San Diego stadium was built, looking much like its peers in many other cities at that time.

One impulse behind the floating stadium proposal for San Diego – to take advantage of the waterfront as a way to generate new urban territory for construction, especially in cities where density and transport issues complicated potential stadia construction – is no stranger than many of the realised urban renewal projects of the 1960s. There are indeed cities all around the world with formerly active industrial waterfronts where such a development could make sense. And yet, there is only one example that I know of that attempts to take advantage of the water in any way akin to what Hilton proposed. The Float at Marina Bay in Singapore, opened in 2007, inverts the proposal of its predecessor from over 40 years earlier, with the stands on terra firma and the pitch floating in Marina Bay. Smaller in scale, with seating for 30,000, Marina Bay hints at the possibilities of exploiting urban waterfronts, but hardly rises to the level of the San Diego proposal.[9] As we will see in Chapter 5, on the future of the stadium, the search for ways to find and aggregate buildable space in dense urban areas may well be the defining challenge for the stadium over the next 50 years. If so, then revisiting the ambitions of Barron Hilton, albeit for different reasons, may be the first step.

The changing fan base

By the late 1960s the world of sport and the experience of the stadium were undergoing a series of changes that would shape the face of sporting architecture for years to come. There were demographic changes afoot, with the rising influence of the post-World War II generation on sport and fan culture. Although grounds in many parts of the world were still overwhelmingly male-dominated spaces, there was a growing presence of women in stadia (as well as other parts of the public sphere). While the increase on this front was in many cases more about magnitude of change rather than overall numbers, it went hand in hand with the growing tendency to view spectatorship of sporting events and stadia in general as a part of the burgeoning consumer culture in capitalist democracies. The growing influence of television was also beginning to shape not just how sport was seen by people away from the grounds, but also how stadia sought to adapt to broadcast media in order to further the economic ambitions of their owners and operators. Last but not least, the persistence of hooliganism and crowd violence played an important part in shaping perceptions about sport, its spectators and the spaces in which the two came together. Hooliganism would exert an especially powerful impact on stadia in the 1980s and 1990s, as we will see later.[10]

Most observers tend to see a mutually beneficial relationship between overall social prosperity and the fortunes of the stadium. But this is not always the case historically, or necessarily so at present. The rising prosperity in cities in the 1960s did not always equal greater opportunities for stadium construction or renovation. The growth of other outlets for consumer entertainment and spending meant that stadia could be perceived (often correctly) as less desirable, less comfortable and less safe destinations for leisure and entertainment. Just as stadia at present have to compete with home technology that was unimaginable 20 years ago, so it was in the 1960s, when television, movie theatres and a whole host of other alternatives vied for the public's disposable income. A hard seat exposed to the elements and sub-par restroom facilities might not dissuade the hard-core fan, but it wasn't going to draw in new ones in such an environment. The challenge going forward was to find a new public face for stadia amidst the changing marketplace of consumer activity into which sport was increasingly being drawn.[11]

An additional challenge for the building type, especially in the USA, was the growth of suburbs and the hollowing out of city cores. This meant it was often no longer obvious where to situate a stadium as the spectators that would populate it were now spread across a larger geography than in previous decades. Site planning became more complicated, as suburban grounds required parking lots ample enough to accommodate the vehicles that carried 45,000+ fans to the game. Suburban stadia also had to provide the amenities that urban stadia could depend on neighbouring bars and restaurants to provide. In the American context, this was part of the story behind the rise of 'tailgating' as a precursor to the game itself. Tailgating, or informal grilling and drinking around an automobile, often takes place over several hours before a game and demands ample parking. Less often remarked on, suburban stadia also had to provide less advertised back-of-house services such as holding pens and, in some cases, even court space for fans who were arrested at games for a variety of reasons.

In the United Kingdom and many parts of Europe, the 1960s were the start of a long period of decline in stadia construction and, even more critically, maintenance. This trend of deferred maintenance would come to play an important role in many of the stadia tragedies of the decades to follow. Although in the American context there was a concerted effort on the part of professional sport leagues and team owners to grow the middle-class fan base at the stadium, there was no real equivalent effort in other parts of the world. In the UK in particular, if anything, stadia were catering to an increasingly working-class fan base. The lack of investment, paired with this narrowing fan base, led in many cases to a political judgement about stadia and those who were to be found in them – a tension that Conservative politicians like Margaret Thatcher would later exploit. In such a formulation, stadia were places of working-class gathering, occasional unrest and uncouth behaviour. While perhaps accurate in some ways, this stereotyping had a deeply pernicious effect. It went hand in hand with declining oversight on the part of civil authorities over public safety and welfare at stadia. In fact, by the 1980s, the issue of public safety at a stadium was almost exclusively defined as the effort to control hooliganism rather than concern for the physical environment of the stadium and surrounding areas.

This was not just a trend in the UK unfortunately, and its true impact would come to light in the form of stadium disasters at Heysel and Hillsborough, among others. The enmity attached to the stadium and its inhabitants could and did spread to the city as a whole on occasion, as in the early 1980s when the Thatcher government considered abandoning the city of Liverpool to a state of 'managed decline'.[12] This sensibility was a major anchor on any aspiration to raise the level of design and performance for stadia. Perversely, the conditions it helped spawn would later play a role in the explosive growth in revenue for leagues and newly built stadia at the turn of the century. The building and security reforms put in place after Hillsborough were a key element in the radical transformation of the culture and design of sporting grounds and the transformation of football into a far more expensive pastime in the 1990s and 2000s.

3   1970–1990: 'Machines for Sports', Disasters and Dramatic Change

The multi-purpose dome

The trend towards domed and multi-purpose stadia that emerged in the 1960s accelerated and spread in the following decades, with often egregious results for fans and spectators. In the United States multi-purpose venues were generally designed to accommodate both baseball and American football. The solution that was most commonly arrived at in the 1970s was a circular concrete stadium, more often than not domed. This form was less than ideal for either sport for a variety of reasons. One problem was that seating, designed to accommodate two pitches of different sizes and shapes, resulted in an arrangement satisfactory to neither set of spectators. Distance from the pitch was maximised, to the detriment of the game-day experience. Home team advantage, often a product of noise and the intimidation of the crowd, also suffered. Another trend from the era that many began to regret almost as soon as it emerged in the USA was the widespread adoption of artificial turf, whether the stadium in question was domed (and thus required it) or not. The hegemony of artificial turf in the 1970s was inescapable – every new stadium built in the USA in that decade had it. Whether you were in Miami or Seattle, you were greeted by the same sterile plastic pitch.

The ubiquity of artificial pitches spoke to a problematic trend of homogenisation in stadia in general in the United States. Team owners and city officials in the 1970s largely spoke with one voice about the possibilities and benefits of multi-purpose, circular, domed stadia as tools for urban regeneration. As one economist commenting on that era noted, 'City leaders have been prepared to go to any length' to keep a team in their city.[13] The result was a boon for team owners who did not hesitate to ask for and receive generous public subsidies for their new home grounds. What was good for the team, however, was not always great for the progress of the building type or the experience of the fan. As Roger Angell, noted American author and frequent writer on sport, lamented: 'More and more these stadia remind one of motels or airports in their perfect and dreary usefulness . . . they are no longer parks but machines for sports.'[14] Le Corbusier's optimistic vision of housing transformed by modern architecture's promise into 'machines for living' was inverted into a telling critique of the placelessness of so many stadia at the time. As another writer complained, the stadia of the 1970s were 'superficially attractive yet "soulless" heaps of steel and concrete'.[15]

The impact on cities of the rise of generic stadia was exacerbated by the twin trend of abandonment

19 Roosevelt Memorial Stadium, Jersey City, New Jersey, a stadium whose decline and eventual demolition presaged the ever-decreasing lifespan of American stadia at the start of the twenty-first century.

and/or demolition of older, more site-specific grounds. The scale and mass of stadia means that, when left in a state of decline, they can become poignantly beautiful ruins. Two memorable cases illustrate how neglect and decline can lead to a condition of beautiful decay. The first of these is Roosevelt Memorial Stadium in New Jersey (Christian H. Ziegler, 1937).

The stadium was completed during the Great Depression under the auspices of President Franklin D. Roosevelt's Works Progress Administration (and named in his honour). Ziegler's design emphasised stripped neo-classicism with touches of art deco as well, reflecting the popularity of both styles in the 1930s. In addition to its formal qualities, Roosevelt Memorial Stadium was also the ground where Jackie Robinson played with the Montreal Royals, a farm team for the Dodgers, in 1946, breaking organised

baseball's colour barrier.[16] A year later, this time with the Dodgers, Robinson would become the first African American player in Major League Baseball. However, neither of these achievements were powerful enough to stem the economic decline of the stadium that began in the 1970s and culminated in its demolition in 1985. Today a housing development occupies the site (a fate not too dissimilar from Archibald Leitch's Ayresome Park in Middlesbrough a decade later). Memorial Stadium opened in Baltimore in 1921, with a major renovation and enlargement in 1949. Home to both Major League Baseball (the Orioles) and National Football League (the Colts) teams, it was a vast project – centre field was 445 feet long. In the mid-1980s, however, the owner of the Colts, dissatisfied with conditions at the ground and a city council unwilling to bankroll renovations on his behalf, packed up his team in the middle of the night and

20   Roosevelt Memorial Stadium, beauty in decay.

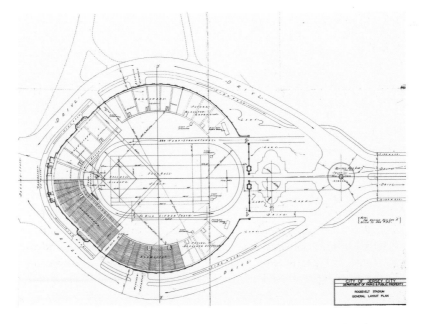

21   Roosevelt Memorial Stadium was an ambitious plan that accommodated baseball, American football and a running track, all in a symmetrical composition.

22   Baltimore Memorial Stadium, Maryland, once home to
two professional teams, also fell into decline.

23 Baltimore Memorial Stadium, the eerie sublime of an empty ground.

decamped for Indiana, a harbinger of the future for many American cities and stadia. The Orioles left not long after, and the stadium endured an era of decline before being demolished in the early 2000s.

The situation in Europe and South America, although different, was not necessarily better. Multi-use stadia were also common, although rarely did they combine baseball and football. Instead, many stadia, especially those built for Olympics and other massive multi-sport events, had both a pitch and a space for athletics, meaning, among other things, a regulation running track circling the pitch. Domed stadia, although far more common in the USA, were also found in Europe and Asia. The tendency to build concrete bowls was as ubiquitous in other parts of the world, however, as it was in the United States. The prevailing mood among designers was towards universalisation of design: what solved a problem in one place (or what was imagined to have solved the problem) was expected to solve it just as adequately somewhere else. However, the problem

24 Baltimore Memorial Stadium, the peculiar effect of creative destruction in the life of American stadia.

with keeping a regulation track in a stadium whose legacy use will be primarily football is the same as found in multi-purpose venues in the United States: the spectators' distance from the pitch and the game played on it. As well known as this shortcoming is, it is one that has not yet been resolved. The transformation of the 2012 London Olympic Stadium into West Ham's home ground in 2016 kept the running track intact, with entirely predictable results. Fans complained about the viewsheds, the atmosphere of the ground was underwhelming, and home fans, less than captivated by the game, took to fighting not with opposing fans, but with each other. The situation became so dire that one stadium designer told the BBC that the whole thing should be demolished and rebuilt as a proper, custom-designed football stadium.[17]

Stadia disasters

The rise of the beautiful stadium in the last two decades is of course notable in part when set against the long trend of pedestrian projects in the preceding years. However, the ubiquity of disappointing design was, unfortunately, the least of the real problems that plagued stadia in the period between 1970 and 1990. The other force shaping these three decades was far worse – fatal disasters. The 1960s drew to a close with the memories of two disasters: Lima in 1964 and Kayseri Atatürk in 1967. Both are surprisingly little mentioned today, in spite of the fact that the tragedy at Lima's Estadio Nacional remains the deadliest stadium disaster in the history of football. Although these two disasters and those in the decades that followed were unique in the scale and scope of their lethality, they were sadly alike in their cause – significant disinvestment in the maintenance and updating of older stadia, neglect on the part of public authorities to modernise their crowd management and policing protocols for game day at grounds that routinely saw 40,000+ spectators, and a generalised contempt among stadium operators for prioritising public safety.

All of these factors were at play in the Lima disaster. In late May of that year Peru faced

Argentina in a decisive home game that the hosts needed to win in order for the national team to make it to the Tokyo Summer Olympic Games. Unfortunately for the hosts, Argentina scored first, a result that if it held meant Peru would not be represented in Tokyo later that year. With six minutes of normal time remaining, Peru appeared to equalise, only for the referee to whistle for a foul and disallow the goal. The crowd of some 53,000, nearly all Peruvian fans, erupted in anger. A handful of those fans made it onto the pitch in protest and were summarily attacked by the Peruvian police who were supposedly there to maintain order. These developments further incited the onlooking fans, who reacted by throwing a range of objects, including bricks torn from the stadium itself, at the police. In response the police made a choice that sealed the fate of hundreds of innocent people that day – they launched tear gas into the north stand. This measure, meant ostensibly to quell the unrest, unsurprisingly had the opposite effect. Fans trying to escape the gas poured into the exit tunnels. These, however, were locked during game time, a fact the police certainly would have known.

Panic spread among the fans, and the crush that it fuelled killed at least 328 people, before the gates eventually buckled and fell under the weight of bodies being pushed against them. As fans were finally released into the streets, a riot broke out which the police outside the stadium, operating with no greater tactical sense than their counterparts inside the ground, tried to stop by firing into the crowd, killing perhaps dozens more. Today there is no reliable accounting of the events of that day, there is no accurate record of those killed, and there has been no sincere effort to hold those responsible for the tragedy to account. Only one person served any jail time as a result – the chief of police who ordered the firing of the tear gas. He served 30 months. The desire of the authorities to evade any responsibility for the event, or even to have the public remember it at all, is evidenced at the ground. After the disaster, seating was reduced by 11,000. Today there is not even a plaque at the Estadio Nacional to commemorate the events of that day, an act of attempted historical erasure that speaks volumes about the collective guilt of the political leadership of Peru in that time.

The drumbeat of disasters in the years that followed was depressingly predictable. Violence between fans of Kayserispor and Sivasspor at a match at the Ataturk Stadium led to the deaths of 43 and injured, depending on media reports, between 300 and 600. It was, regrettably, a harbinger of more to come. In 1971, at an Old Firm game between Celtic and Rangers at Ibrox Park in Glasgow, crowded conditions on an exit stairway contributed to a crush at the end of the match that claimed the lives of 66 and injured more than 200. Three years later, a stampede at the Zamalek Stadium in Cairo during a friendly match between Egyptian and Czech clubs left at least 48 dead and 50 injured.

It was the 1980s, however, that witnessed the deadliest sequence of stadia disasters in the post-World War II era. I have vivid memories of the coverage of those events, especially those from the end of the decade. There was something about the accelerating sense of dread that began to accompany sporting news. The labour unrest in the United Kingdom, the anxieties and ambiguities of the Cold War that shaped (or deformed) the 1980, 1984 and even 1988 Summer Olympic Games, and the sense by the end of the decade of an emerging monumental, tectonic shift in the global order all added something ineffable and terrible to the stadium tragedies of the time.

The other aspect of these disasters was their geopolitical variation. Although in public perception stadium disasters are inextricably linked with hooliganism, the truth is more complicated. Similarly, although English fans were singled out for special opprobrium in the 1980s, this was not always borne out by the facts afterwards. The decade opened with the Karaiskakis disaster in Greece when a crowd crush at the conclusion of a match between Olympiacos and AEK Athens killed 21 and injured 55. The cause was not hooliganism, but in all likelihood a door blocking part of the exit stairway at Gate 7 of the stadium. It is the sort of banal detail that in the context of a football match can turn lethal. The following year, in Moscow, a last-minute goal

in a UEFA Cup match between FC Spartak Moscow and HFC Haarlem triggered a stampede in an exit stairway, and the resulting pile-up of bodies killed 66 and injured at least 61, although these figures were only made public years later.

The last half of the 1980s were deadlier than the first, and saw some of the most notorious stadium disasters of the twentieth century, disasters that forever changed the way stadia are designed, the fashion in which they are occupied and the character of public reception of them. The year 1985 saw two terribly lethal stadium disasters separated by only a few weeks. The first was in Bradford, in the United Kingdom, at the Valley Parade Stadium. Valley Parade was built in 1886, in what is often thought of as the 'classic' era of stadium construction in the late nineteenth century. It was at this time that many of the grand stadia in the UK were built, including Highbury (Arsenal), Ibrox Park (Rangers) and Craven Cottage (Fulham). These famous grounds all shared something in common with the less famous Valley Parade – the same architect, Archibald Leitch, designed them all. Tellingly, Leitch was educated in Scotland not as an architect, but as an engineer, and he had originally worked designing factories before moving into the design of stadia. His designs reflect the sensibilities of the late nineteenth and early twentieth centuries in viewing stadia as pragmatic structures that present a series of problems that need to be resolved sensibly and in an efficient, cost-effective fashion.[18]

Leitch designed Ibrox Park, his first stadium, at the age of 34. He had already had a successful career as an engineer, but he found his real calling in designing stadia. It is difficult to overstate Leitch's impact on football grounds in the UK, but the list of clubs on whose behalf he designed entire grounds or stands is telling: Liverpool, Manchester United, Arsenal, Chelsea, Tottenham, Fulham, Crystal Palace and Aston Villa. In all, Leitch had a hand in grounds for 16 First Division clubs by the end of the 1920s. And yet, at his death in 1939, there was little public comment on his passing and his incredible influence on the urban landscape in cities across the UK. This reflected the contemporary view that stadium design was not a grand architectural endeavour, but something much more mundane, and left to a handful of anonymous technical experts.

Such a sensibility prevailed for more than half a century, and helps to explain why Valley Parade in 1985 was in a state of considerable disrepair. It was not age alone. The lack of investment in updating Valley Parade was in no way unique to Bradford City Football Club; in the 1980s it was the norm rather than the exception. Larger, national economic forces were also at play, and hardly helped. These were the years before bumper contracts for broadcast rights flooded English football with cash. Lax public oversight concerning stadium safety procedures and operations played a role (such as allowing smoking, for instance), as did the politics of the Thatcher era that cast most football fans as members of the political opposition. Finally, the largely unchecked authority of club owners to dictate how and in what ways their stadia were maintained and operated meant sometimes wholly inadequate leadership in making potentially life-and-death decisions. Such was the case with Bradford City, where the decision not to replace the wooden roof over the main stand, or to properly maintain the areas under the seating of the main stand, led to a build up of rubbish, with fatal consequences.

Forty minutes into a match between Bradford City and Lincoln City, a fire broke out in the back three rows of the main stand – started when a lit cigarette fell between the floorboards and ignited paper and other match-day debris below. Within four minutes the entire stand was on fire, in a turn of events broadcast on television. Fifty-six people were killed and another 265 injured. It was revealed on the 30th anniversary of the fire that Bradford City's owner at the time of the disaster had a long history of owning businesses that burned down and in return receiving substantial insurance payouts. Further doubts were raised about the lit-cigarette explanation for the origin of the fire. Questions remain about the true cause of the fire and the full responsibility for the lives lost that day.[19]

Later that month another stadium disaster, this one in Belgium, reinforced the sense that the global state of stadia was increasingly a question of public safety at a scale no one had fully grasped. The stadium in question this time, Heysel, is now synonymous with two of the uglier aspects of sport history: fan violence and woefully maintained stadia. An hour before kick-off, Liverpool supporters attacked Juventus fans, causing a scramble of spectators, a crush of bodies, and the collapse of part of the stadium. Unlike Valley Parade, however, Heysel was a national stadium, speaking to the culpability not just of a singly negligent club owner, but to a nation-state. Much of the blame for the tragedy at Heysel in the aftermath of the disaster was directed at the away fans – Liverpool supporters – and English clubs were hit with a five-year ban from European competition. Liverpool had one additional year added to the ban, leaving the club facing a six-year caesura from European competition, which had formerly been one of the club's areas of greatest success. And yet, while individual Liverpool fans certainly behaved unacceptably, and were properly brought to trial, neither Belgium nor UEFA were ever held to account for their roles in the tragedy.

In many of the stadium disasters of this period, a failure of accountability before and after the event was the order of the day. At a football match in Kathmandu, Nepal, in March 1988 a hailstorm broke out (an unfortunately common weather event there). The Dasarath Stadium, the national stadium of Nepal, had open stands on three sides, and the capacity crowd of some 30,000 understandably moved en masse to the exits. The authorities at the stadium, however, had locked all but one of the eight exits. Crushes at the locked gates killed 93 people (reported figures in the West vary, as Nepal was at that time a monarchy with a government-operated media). Although the stadium was (and is) owned by the government of Nepal, no restitution was made to the families of the victims who died that day.

The 1980s ended as they had begun, with a final disaster, one that would spur dramatic changes in the design and operation of stadia in the UK and around the world: Hillsborough. In addition to Hillsborough's impact on stadium design, it has also shaped public trust in governmental authorities and their stewardship of public safety. The facts of the disaster itself are well known now only after 27 years of legal battles and therefore bear repeating. An FA Cup semi-final between Liverpool and Nottingham Forest was played at a neutral ground: Sheffield Wednesday's Hillsborough Stadium. Built in 1899, Hillsborough had last been meaningfully updated for the 1966 World Cup. It was ill suited to what was to be a heavily attended and high-intensity event like an FA Cup semi-final tie for a number of reasons. The approach to the ground for Liverpool fans, who were segregated to the west and north stands, was squeezed between the River Don and Leppings Lane, creating bottleneck conditions as fans reached the ground. Fans arriving without tickets swelled the numbers trying to move through the turnstiles. Once fans made it through this first obstacle to safe and measured ingress into the ground, they were confronted with another design flaw, a tunnel that funnelled spectators to two pens behind the goal. These filled quickly, highlighting a third major problem. Hillsborough was a fenced ground, meaning that high metal fences ran around the pitch at the base of the seating areas. Meant to deter pitch invasions, these also had the effect of acting as deadly barriers to those at the front of the pens behind the goal. As spectators were tunnelled into the pens at the rear, people were pushed forward, pressing up against the spectators stuck between the crowd behind them and the fencing in front of them.

Fencing also ran between the pens, making movement by the fans into the largely empty pens adjacent to 3 and 4 impossible. Fearing a riot outside the gates, the police opened up exit gates to allow more fans to rush in as the game neared kick-off, exacerbating the situation inside the ground. Police efforts at the stadium that day were focused on the prevention of hooliganism rather than public safety, a reflection of the two-fold reality of football's more working-class fan base at the time and the larger national tensions between the UK's Conservative government and working-class bastions like the city of Liverpool. As a result, efforts to manage the flow of fans in a more reasoned manner in order to prevent a crush were ignored, with tragic consequences. Ninety-six people died as a result of

the crush that took place. Another 766 were injured. The youngest to die was a ten-year-old boy, the oldest was 67.[20]

A disregard for fundamental safety elements was also behind the 1992 Armand Cesari Stadium disaster in Corsica. The Cesari Stadium is home to SC Bastia, who were then playing in the Second Division in the French Football League. On 5 May 1992, SC Bastia were to play a semi-final match in the Coupe de France against Olympique de Marseille, a much larger and more famous club from the upper tier of French football. Seeking to capitalise on the match, SC Bastia's board decided to build a temporary grandstand for 10,000 people to accommodate more ticketholders. The construction was shoddy and local building authorities appeared to offer no oversight or guidance on the temporary stand, which collapsed minutes before kick-off was scheduled. In total 18 people were killed and more than 2,300 were injured. As with Hillsborough and Heysel before, accountability after that tragedy was in short supply, and poor construction methods coupled with overcrowding continued to be a problem for stadia and spectators around the world into the first decades of the twenty-first century.

Ambitious projects of the 1970s–1990s

The three decades in question were, at least as far as stadia are concerned, defined by twin trends towards homogeneity and tragedy. These are both indicators of the lack of critical thinking around stadia during those years, an absence felt not just in lacklustre design but also in a tragic loss of life. Nevertheless, a number of projects emerged in this period that were exceptions to these trends. Some of these are indisputably architecturally ambitious in a way that distinguishes them from their peers. Others are of note because of the deployment of novel technologies or because their use of scale is particularly noteworthy. It is worth mentioning that almost all of the examples from the United States have since been demolished, a fact that highlights the much briefer lifespans of stadia in the USA relative to the rest of the world.

25   Omni Coliseum, Atlanta, Georgia, was ambitious, novel in design, a driver of urban development, and also a victim of the wrecking ball.

Omni Coliseum

Among those demolished projects, the Omni Coliseum in Atlanta was both structurally and visually interesting. A novel structural system for the roof, which many commentators thought resembled an egg crate, was clad in Cor-Ten steel, giving the structure arresting elevations and perspectives. The heaviness of the weathered steel was contrasted at the corners of the arena by multi-storey glazing. Seating in the interior, in order to maximise the compact site, was rotated to run from corner to corner. The Coliseum, designed by the Atlanta-based firm of Tvsdesign, was intended to spur downtown real estate development (indeed, the client for the Omni was a large real estate developer), and to

that end it was a success. Less successful were the teams that played in the Omni and the performance of some of the building materials themselves, particularly the exterior steel, which weathered much faster than anticipated. Just 15 years after it opened, the Omni was demolished. It is a narrative that would be repeated time and again in the USA.

Kingdome

Perhaps one reason so many stadia in the USA from this era were relatively short-lived is that so many of them were built in cities that aspired to be players on a larger stage and, in many of those cities, business leaders and politicians agreed that a new stadium was a sure path to the ascent they

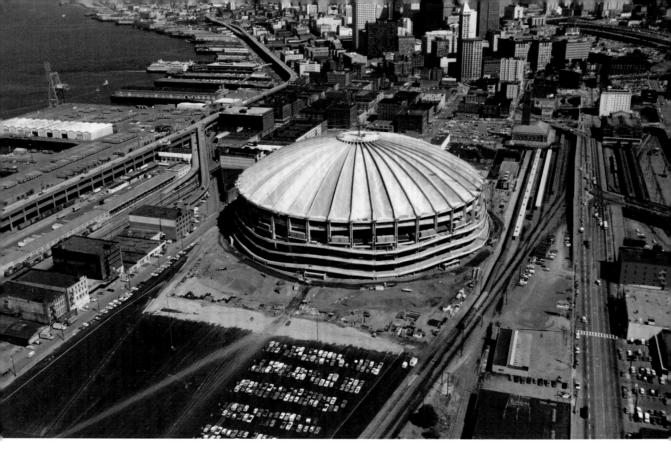

26　Kingdome, Seattle, Washington, was not too big to fail.

craved. This was certainly the case in Seattle, where the massive, perhaps monstrous, Kingdome was built after more than a decade of lobbying by local business owners in spite of widespread disinterest among voters in such a project. As is often the case, when business leaders are lobbying for something that city leaders also want, the opinion of voters does not hold sway over time, and in 1976 Seattle found itself the proud owner of a domed, multi-purpose concrete stadium. What made the Kingdome novel was both its formal qualities, limited though they were, and the mode of its demise.

Although many concrete-domed stadia in the USA had relatively anonymous qualities aside from their size, the Kingdome had a number of striking elements. The first was the stacked tiers of undulating circulation that wrapped the building and the contrasting undulating circulation on the interior. These combined to give the building a

much more lightweight and possibly even playful quality than most structures of its scale possessed. The second was the roof, which was elegantly ribbed and appeared strikingly lightweight, belying its concrete construction. Finally, the Kingdome exploited its size via night-time illumination in a way few other stadia of the time did (or do today for that matter). The Kingdome, like many multi-purpose domed stadia, fell into disrepair over time, as maintenance costs were higher than anticipated. In the case of the Kingdome, the roof leaked from the outset, particularly problematic in the rainy Seattle climate. A series of very public failures of the roof in the early 1990s led the owners of the Major League Baseball and National Football League teams that played in the Kingdome to threaten to relocate cities rather than stay in the venue. By the late 1990s the fate of the building was sealed. In early 2000 the Kingdome was imploded, making it at the time the largest building ever demolished in that fashion. The demolition was newsworthy enough to be covered live by the sports network ESPN. Incredibly, it would be another 15 years before the bonds that financed the Kingdome were paid off.

Munich 1972 Olympic Stadium

In an era rich in cookie-cutter projects, the most memorable stadium was built in Munich for the 1972 Summer Olympic Games. Designed by Behnisch & Partner with assistance from Frei Otto, the Olympiastadion is a dramatic example of the formal possibilities of Otto's architecture of tensile structures. The Olympiastadion was part of a larger complex of tent-like structures at the Olympiapark, adding to the spectacular character of the canopies made of thousands of square metres of acrylic glass and hundreds of miles of steel cables that form the tent-like enclosures that dot the grounds. The Olympiastadion's seating did resemble a classical

stadion, set as it was into the sides of an earthen bowl. This meant the stadium did not loom over the rest of the city. This did not assuage locals, many of whom objected to its modernist character. The transparency of the canopies and the absence of any references to the neo-classical historical forms and elements common to the buildings of the 1936 Berlin Summer Olympics were intended to highlight the character of a new, democratic and open West Germany.

The stadium was and remains an incredibly ambitious project, but one whose aspirations were tragically undermined by a terrorist attack in the second week of the Games. Eight armed Palestinians, who were members of Black September, took eleven Israeli athletes and coaches hostage. The rescue effort was a disastrous failure; all eleven Israelis were killed, as were five of the eight members of Black September, along with one West German police officer. The attack led

27   Olympiastadion, Munich, Germany, built for the 1972 Olympics, still looks sharp today.

28 Olympiastadion, designed to be a symbol of an open, democratic (then) West Germany, it was also the site of a terrorist attack.

to a dramatic shift in the management of future Games, with security taking on a central role in their planning and execution. The role of security in the Games and stadia that Munich brought to the public eye would only increase in subsequent years. In spite of all of this historical baggage, the Olympiastadion today is a popular attraction for tourists and Munich residents alike.

Montreal 1976 Olympic Stadium

The Summer Olympic Games were the driver for the construction of another formally audacious project that was also an exemplar of nearly every potential political, economic and technical negative externality associated with stadia. In 1970 the International Olympic Committee awarded the 1976 Summer Olympic Games to the city of Montreal over competing bids from Los Angeles and Moscow. The political leadership of the city cast the awarding of the Olympics as proof that Montreal had achieved the status of a global city. Backers of the Olympic bid also insisted that the Games would be modest and affordable – a claim that foreshadowed the debacle that was to come. Roger Taillibert, a French architect, was chosen to design the Olympic Village and its signature element, the Olympic Stadium. Taillibert was, by all accounts, a reasonable choice – he had, just a few years earlier, been chosen to design the Parc des Princes Stadium in Paris and, perhaps just as important, had a francophone and cosmopolitan flair in keeping with Montreal's own.

29   Montreal 1976 Olympic Stadium, Canada, a soaring design that took 30 years to pay for and became a symbol of Olympic excess.

The design Taillibert developed for the Olympic Stadium called for a vast concrete bowl with articulated ribs that bore a slight resemblance to the Parc des Princes. Unlike the Parc des Princes, however, this project also called for the world's tallest inclined tower to be located at one end of the stadium. It was from this tower that an array of steel cables would support the retractable roof for the stadium, a critical feature for legacy use in the snowy climate of the city. Any project of this scale and structural complexity demands careful planning and management, and unfortunately Montreal's political leaders and the city's Olympic backers offered little of either. This failure was compounded by the fractious relationship between city leadership and the labour unions whose participation was critical to the success or failure of the project. Construction delays (some caused by labour strikes and others by winter weather), cost overruns and weak oversight plagued the Olympic Stadium from the start. Taillibert was removed from the project in the year before the Games, but this did not solve the problem, as the architect was not the principal stumbling block. Construction was not completed before the opening ceremonies – it was suspended. In fact, construction on the stadium would continue for years after the Olympics. Work on the roof, which never operated as intended, continued for decades, with plans for a replacement roof under consideration as recently as 2017.

The management of the construction of Taillibert's stadium, and perhaps even the aspiration for a retractable roof in the snow-heavy climate of Montreal, was poor. The management of the financing for the project and the Games as a whole was catastrophic. Backers of Montreal's bid insisted that the Olympics would make the city money. Instead, the final cost of the Games came in at an eye-watering 13 times the original projections. The stadium alone, which currently has no permanent tenants, cost $1.1 billion. Paying off the Games took the city nearly 30 years, involved the levy of a special tax in order to generate revenue, and drained resources away from other municipal causes. In the decades after the Olympics, and as the city was paying off stadium debt, the tower caught fire, the roof failed repeatedly, leading to emergency closures, and – the ultimate indignity – the main tenants, the Montreal Expos, decamped to Washington, DC. Montreal is today widely regarded as a nadir in Olympic history, perhaps only supplanted by the aftermath of the 2004 Athens Games, whose cost contributed to the Greek debt crisis that began to unfold in 2008.

SESC Pompeia

Another significant project from the era, the SESC Pompeia, is not properly a stadium, but a sport tower. It is included here nevertheless because it is one of the more novel sport architecture projects of the time, and it remains less well known than it should be. Designed by Lina Bo Bardi and opened in 1986 in São Paulo, Brazil, the SESC Pompeia is a marvellous space formed by the adaptive reuse of an old steel barrel manufacturing facility with the addition of several monumental concrete structures. This multi-purpose facility includes swimming facilities, indoor football pitches and racquet sport courts, all housed in a large tower linked to the original factory via bridges that zig-zag through the air. The aim of Bo Bardi and her team at the

30   SESC Pompeia, São Paulo, Brazil, not a stadium in the conventional sense, it nevertheless was one of the most imaginative works of sport architecture in the twentieth century.

31   SESC Pompeia, showing the famous punched apertures, one of the project's
many peculiar and wonderful features.

SESC Pompeia was to encourage the recreational practice of sport. As a result, the pools and the court spaces are not proportioned in conformance with national federation standards, meaning they cannot be used for competitive events. Instead, they are there for local residents to enjoy according to their respective skill levels. The reinforced concrete provides one powerful sense of visual identity for the project; the other is the window openings in the main volume which look as if they were punched through the walls by hand and hammer. At the time Bo Bardi was finishing the SESC Pompeia, Brazil was just emerging from two decades of rule by a military dictatorship. The Italian-born Bo Bardi, who had emigrated to Brazil several decades earlier, developed an architectural language at the SESC Pompeia that diverged dramatically from the heavy-handed state-approved styles of the dictators' favoured designers. Programmatically, it also spoke to Bo Bardi's lifelong interest in architecture that

served a social need as well as a degree of aesthetic refinement. It is a powerful reminder that sport architecture, far from being removed from the core values that societies around the world grapple with, is often squarely in the middle of them.

John Smith's Stadium

A last highlight from an era often defined as one of doom and gloom is the John Smith's Stadium in Huddersfield, UK (HOK Sport, now Populous, 1994), which has had various monikers since its opening. The design for the stadium at Huddersfield emerged from Populous' theoretical project called the 'Stadium for the Nineties'. This research project sought to imagine how the next generation of stadia would evolve and advance the technical, formal and social aspects of the building type. Inspired by the premise of a multi-faceted project, Populous proposed that the stadium would serve as what the firm calls a 'social oasis' that in turn would attract additional leisure and retail development. The programme for the stadium therefore was not restricted to existing norms, and included a hotel, a half Olympic pool and a diving tank. The defining formal features of the project are the arched trusses that carry the seating coverage for each of the stands, the longest of which spans 140 metres. In recognition of the advances Populous made with the John Smith's Stadium, it was awarded the 'Building of the Year Award' from the Royal Institute of British Architects (RIBA) in 1995.

The RIBA award for Huddersfield's stadium suggested the turn that the building type, especially at the elite level, would take in the first two decades of the twenty-first century. The turn towards design as a matter of developing club identity and as a technique for increasing revenues led to ever-more advanced designs. It also saw a shift in the number and character of firms involved in stadia design around the world. This change was important not only because it drew new design firms into the world of stadia, but also because it drew new clients into the fold to pay for a more refined degree of design and construction. These clients came from the expected places – the wealthiest leagues in the biggest cities – but also

32   Huddersfield Town Stadium, UK, a project that sought to propel the thinking about stadia forward and winner of the Royal Institute of British Architects' Building of the Year Award.

from cities and locales that in the past had not been centres of stadia construction. This would transform not just the building type, but the new locales into which it would be introduced.

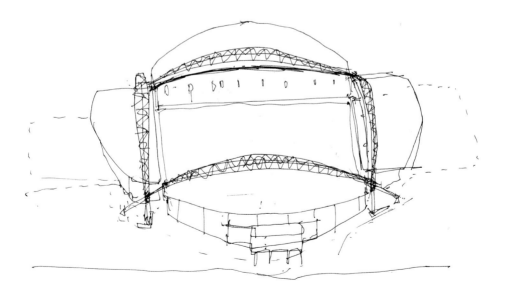

33   Huddersfield Town Stadium, the monumental arched trusses as an iconic feature.

4   2000 to Present: The Rise of the Architect Stadium

Why study and write about stadia apart from the question of the games played in them? It is a question I get quite often, especially from my fellow architects and architectural historians. Perhaps one way to answer is to compare two recent grand public projects in a major American city – a museum and a stadium in Los Angeles. If you compare the number of paragraphs written about each project's meaning and significance, those written about the museum – the Broad, designed by Diller, Scofidio + Renfro – dwarf those written about the new stadium for the Los Angeles Rams, an American football team. This is in spite of the fact that the museum cost around $140 million and the stadium will cost at least $2.6 billion.

Rather, it is that critics and the general public alike expect a museum, as a building type and programme, to be the sort of architecture that has something significant to say about the culture and society from which it emerges. And that something is generally presumed to be normative and positive. This is in spite of the fact that any reasonably educated architect who went to school after 1990 should be familiar with the powerful critique of museums by any number of post-structuralist critics, most importantly Michel Foucault, who identified the museum as a space of power and hegemony. Indeed, any museum visitor who is reasonably well educated in the liberal arts should know more or less the same. And yet, no one suggests that it is inappropriate to treat the museum as an exalted architectural exercise that merits scrutiny.

The stadium, on the other hand, receives far less attention in this regard. Even many of the most ardent supporters of a club might not have the slightest idea who was behind the design of their home ground. This is notable, especially in the American context, as stadia often receive substantial public funding. Across the United States locales that are cutting funding for the arts, art education and museums are spending hundreds of millions of dollars on stadia. This is not just antipathy to the arts and love for sport. Many of these same cities and locales are also cutting funding for athletics, public parks and even physical education programmes for youth. How is it that politicians and voters across geographies and political spectrums can converge on defunding of the arts while at the same time subsidising professional sports stadia? I argue that the failure to examine stadia as a building type deserving of the same careful consideration as the museum does not render that building type less powerful – indeed, it redoubles its hegemony.

This book is not intended to criticise the presence of stadia, or even their public funding per se. It is instead an effort to treat the building type with the same sustained degree of attention as other building types, and to say that we can read as much about a society's values, or the values of its ruling class, by examining its stadium as we can by looking at its libraries, city halls, palaces or cathedrals.

34   New Wembley, London, taking the monumental truss as identifying feature to new, even greater heights.

'Upgrading' stadia

The first decade of the twenty-first century opened with the news that Wembley Stadium in London would close. The iconic venue, well known not just in the United Kingdom but around the world, was to be demolished, and replaced by a modern, high-tech stadium designed by Sir Norman Foster. It was in many respects a harbinger of what was to come over the next two decades. Historic grounds, both iconic and less so, were to be retired and replaced by newer, more advanced and substantially more expensive venues. In the case of Wembley, the original 1923 stadium, built at a cost of £750,000 (roughly £39 million in 2017), was replaced with one that cost £789 million (or just over £1 billion in 2017). Even adjusting for inflation, that is a monumental change in cost, especially considering the demolished Wembley could hold 127,000 and the new one only closer to 90,000. The thinking that drove the decision to demolish and replace Wembley was not unique to that venue, and the forces that remade the thinking about stadia in the twenty-first century are worth exploring in order to understand how

35 New Wembley, the view of the interior.

we arrived at the present moment when stadia are often the largest, most complex and most expensive building projects in whatever city in the world one finds them.

For much of the twentieth century a fairly single-minded economic model drove the formal qualities of stadia: more seats equalled more revenue. So, if a club wanted to increase its profits, as one noted architect of stadia observes, the most common path to that was to build larger stands and sell more tickets.[21] The formal aspirations of stadia were secondary in most cases to economic ones. This is not to say formal ambitions didn't also exist; as we

(*right*) 36 New Wembley arch: many of the structural elements have an almost constructivist quality to them.

have seen in the previous chapters, they certainly did. But they were rarely front and centre. This too was a reflection of the reality that most of those 'bums in seats' belonged to working-class and middle-class men, and most club owners presumed they were interested in paying for sport more than design. Whether this is true I think is up for debate, but that was the prevailing mode of thought across an otherwise surprisingly varied geography.

As the second decade of the twenty-first century draws to a close, it is tempting to imagine that the explosion of spectacular stadia projects designed by world-renowned architects means that formal ambitions have supplanted mere economic ones. That, however, would be a mistake. Instead, a shift in the economic model of stadia is driving this transformation, and this one is increasingly global as well. Whether you are in Atlanta watching an American football game at Mercedes-Benz Stadium (HOK, 2017) or in London watching Spurs at their new stadium (Populous, expected late 2018), the goal for the designers is two-fold and largely the same: to get people to leave the comfort of their home and high-definition, large-screen televisions, and then to extract as much money from them as possible while they are at the ground. Rather than trying to sell more tickets, clubs are now interested in attracting a cohort of ticket holders who will pay not just for a ticket, but also for a whole host of other amenities.

Spectacle is the tool to get people to the ground, and then a radical reimagining of what the programme of the stadium can contain is the means for profitability. The results are often visually stunning exteriors – see the aforementioned projects. The quest for spectacle also extends into the forms of the interiors and the character of how those spaces are to be used. At the New Spurs Stadium – tellingly referred to on the club's website as a 'world class entertainment venue' – those include a top-tier suite for fans that will provide access via one-way glass to players entering and leaving the pitch, rather than visual access to the game itself. Fans will also have the chance to climb the exterior of the building and skywalk around the lip of the stadium. Design here is a driver to attract spectators and attendance even on days when

37   New Spurs Stadium, Tottenham, London, certain to be renamed after a corporate behemoth before opening day, as is now, sadly, the norm.

no game is played, with additional programmatic changes in the norm for most stadia such as retail, conference facilities, cafes and even a hotel.

The developments in Atlanta and London are hardly unique. Indeed, in London alone in the years since Wembley closed a number of elite football clubs have moved to new grounds or announced plans to build one. Among those, Arsenal not only opened a new stadium in 2006 (Emirates Stadium, Populous) but also redeveloped the ground they moved out of, Highbury, into flats (Highbury Square, Allies and Morrison, 2009), suggesting that substantially more attractive options than demolition exist for stadia that are no longer desirable as sporting venues. West Ham moved into the extensively and expensively remodelled London Olympic Stadium and Chelsea revealed plans for a revamp of Stamford Bridge by Herzog and de Meuron, making the firm perhaps the leader in capital 'A' architecture for sporting venues. The Chelsea project, all brick piers and suggestions of Roman revival arches, will be a radical transformation of the Bridge, and as with the New Spurs Stadium, promises to include amenities to bring in guests year-round. Other major clubs in the UK are following suit, with Liverpool, Everton and Manchester City all either having or in the process of undergoing new construction or major transformations.

(*following pages*) 38   New Spurs Stadium, a twenty-first-century multi-purpose stadium, designed to accommodate both association and American football.

Stadia as a tool for urban regeneration

These cases, and those of other new stadia in the last decade in the USA, point to another reality shaping the architectural attention placed on these projects – the aim to treat stadia as a means of urban regeneration. Although the context of how and in which ways public funds or other resources are deployed to build these structures varies greatly between the United States and the UK and Europe, one element is common across these locales – the idea that stadia and urban regeneration can be successfully linked. In a sense this approach treats the stadium as something akin to an anchor tenant – the project that will attract future development that will lead to a neighbourhood's socio-economic revival. As large-scale funding from central governments for urban redevelopment has declined under neo-liberal governments in power over the past 30 years, other means of advancing redevelopment have taken its place. The stadium has been a particularly popular tool for attempting to generate positive urban change.[22]

The additional obligations and possible outcomes attached to new stadia as a result mean their appearance is a more weighty matter than when they were largely inward-looking projects alone. If they are to anchor redevelopment, then they must be able to be situated more thoughtfully into the urban fabric, must have activities associated with them for more than game day alone, and must take into account how important public relations will be to their success or failure as engines of change and redevelopment. The industrial-style architecture of many stadia and the elevations it produces simply aren't compatible with such an agenda. As such, the iconic but hardly 'beautiful' elevations of an Old Trafford or the unloved contours of the concrete bowls born in the 1960s and 1970s are not options when the goal is more than simply hosting game-day activities.

39   Emirates Stadium, Holloway, London, the stadium that is as much part of
Arsene Wenger's legacy at Arsenal as the beautiful football he championed

The new wave of stadium design

Three intertwined factors converged in the first decades of the twenty-first century to produce a whole range of novel, innovative and formally audacious projects: 1. The need for clubs to compete with increasing availability of games across an array of digital platforms in the comfort of fans' own homes or cars; 2. The desire to keep fans spending their money at ever higher amounts for longer periods of time; and 3. The decision by politicians and club owners to claim that new stadia can serve as agents of urban regeneration. The impetus for these stadia might not rub everyone the right way, but the architectural results are nevertheless often quite stunning. Not all of these projects have been monumental in scale, although many of them are. Not all of them were built in the cities where you would expect to find challenging new architecture, though many of them were. And not all of them were built to house the best-known, most popular

sports in the world, although not surprisingly many were. Nevertheless, this variety suggests that the adoption of the stadium as the signal urban project of the twenty-first century is widespread, although strangely overlooked in the architectural and popular press. More cities in more places are hosting the construction of architecturally significant stadia. Whether this is a bubble about to be pierced when 'peak stadia' is reached remains to be seen. In the meantime, we can enjoy the fruits of the design bar being raised at many if not all of these projects.

Emirates Stadium

We have mentioned two of the early, 'signal' stadium projects of the 2000s: New Wembley and Emirates Stadium, both in London. These are architecturally notable for divergent reasons. New Wembley is a national stadium, freighted with the obligation to host the national team on a sporadic basis rather than a club team on a fixed schedule. It is far larger than most football stadia in contemporary life (even

the mega-sized football stadia of Brazil, Mexico and elsewhere have been scaled down in terms of seats). It was replacing an incredibly iconic structure, and so had to generate a new, iconic presentation from day one, without the benefit of historic matches and occasions that built Old Wembley's reputation over time. In order to accomplish this task, Foster + Partners and Populous, the architects of the project, turned to a variation of Foster's well-established high-tech architectural language. New Wembley is most powerfully defined by the monumental arch that supports all of the north stand roof and part of the south stand. Running 315 metres, it is the longest single-span roof structure in the world and its visual impact is made even greater by the way it tilts off the centre line one would expect the spine of a roof to hold. Brightly illuminated at night, it is a spectacular sight that immediately confirms to the viewer their location in the world. Perhaps as important for our discussion about the bold new world of stadia that the twenty-first century has revealed, New Wembley was also massively over-budget, an early warning that the advances in this building type would not come cheaply.

Arsenal's new stadium, the Emirates, was also a high-tech project, but looking at the ground today, one is more struck by how the Emirates foreshadowed the two elements identified as drivers of novel, architecturally complex architecture in the present century: getting people to the game, and revitalising (or attempting to) the surrounding neighbourhood. Arsenal, like many clubs in older, compact venues, was facing pressure to increase gate receipts for their home games. This task required construction of a new venue, which presents the opportunity for economic growth, but is not without risk. Clubs moving into new, larger grounds almost always face an immediate challenge: will 15,000 more fans show up if you make the space for them? How does one replicate at a new ground the energy and affection that drove attendance at the former ground? Failure to address these concerns increases the likelihood that fans will choose other alternatives to paying to see the game in person, particularly if your club has some of the highest ticket costs in the league.

The strategy was to offer fans at the Emirates a range of hospitality and entertainment options above and beyond that which the famous, but older and cramped, Highbury could. These were placed within a spacious bowl with an undulating upper tier of seating that fits compactly into the borough of Islington. Just as important to the success of the stadium as the elements that organise the interior are the efforts made to keep a stadium that holds some 60,000 spectators at a scale that does not overwhelm its surroundings. Part of the beauty of this project is the way it situates itself into the fabric of the neighbourhood, a concern too often overlooked in other urban stadia projects, particularly in the United States. The venue is programmed to host conferences, with housing deployed around the venue, and with pedestrian access through and across the site of the grounds year-round. From an urban design perspective, the Emirates is a model for how to introduce a monumental building into an existing urban fabric.

Allianz Arena and Beijing 2008 Olympic Stadium

A number of other early signal projects that suggested the rapidly changing character of the stadium followed on the heels of the Emirates. Among the best known are two projects by Herzog and de Meuron: the Allianz Arena in Munich, completed in 2005, and the 2008 Beijing Olympic Stadium. The former is nominally a bowl stadium but wrapped in ETFE pillows. ETFE, or Ethylene Tetrafluoroethylene, is a transparent and lightweight material and it can take on an otherworldly quality, appearing in the day-time like a massive cushioned monolith. The diamond geometry of the ETFE pillows on the Allianz produces a banding effect, with looping horizontal bands and striking diagonal vertical bands giving the impression of cables in tension against an inflated mass. At night, when the ETFE is lit in a range of colours, the building takes on a carnivalesque quality distinct from any other ground in the world.

The second project, widely known as the Bird's Nest, was a collaboration with Chinese artist Ai Wei Wei and is perhaps among the most widely

(*top right*) 40   Allianz Arena, Munich, Germany, perched alongside a highway; its siting is twentieth century, but its form is resolutely forward looking.

(*bottom right*) 41   Allianz Arena, showing the striking exterior wrap of ETFE (Ethylene Tetrafluoroethylene).

43   Beijing 2008 Olympic Stadium, a detail of the exuberant interior spaces.

expression reminiscent of Richard Serra. This stadium, extremely modest in size compared to most in this book, by virtue of the way it operates on its site, transforms nature into landscape. This transformation allows the project to be concerned with more than just addressing programmatic need; it means the building has, as Robert Hughes put it speaking about Mies and his Farnsworth House, 'an idea about the world'.[23]

44   Tossols-Basil Athletics Stadium, Olot, Spain, one of the most ephemeral stadia anywhere in the world.

recognisable stadia in the world. It is a mixture of concrete and steel that recalls brutalist architecture while simultaneously looking like something very much from the future. The Chinese were keen to exploit hosting the Summer Games to show off a vibrant, globally influential state, and to that end wanted an Olympic Stadium that would reflect a new era of ascendancy in the world. The concrete nest, extravagantly lit at night and as much a piece of sculpture as an identifiable stadium, certainly fit the bill. The stadium was relentlessly photographed and became immediately recognisable as a marker of place for the city of Beijing. Although unquestionably striking and beautiful, the Bird's Nest does not have any real legacy use, and so post-Games it is all spectacle and little substance.

Tossols-Basil Athletics Stadium

RCR Arquitectes, who would go on to win the Pritzker Prize in 2017, were behind the Tossols-Basil Athletics Stadium (2000) in Olot, Spain. A marvel of integration of site, programme and materiality – in this case Cor-Ten steel – Tossols stadium is a masterclass of precision and control. The project displays an architectural character that suggests Mies van der Rohe and a sculptural

(*right*) 45   Tossols-Basil Athletics Stadium, the running track and lighting towers touching lightly on the surrounding landscape.

46 Tossols-Basil Athletics Stadium, a conceptual sketch of the lighting towers.

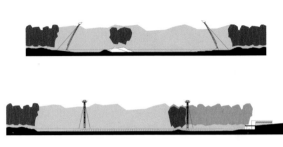

49 Tossols-Basil Athletics Stadium, elevations.

47 Tossols-Basil Athletics Stadium, a conceptual sketch of the small stand at the ground.

50 Tossols-Basil Athletics Stadium, the larger geographical context.

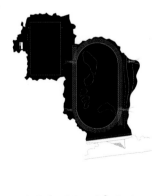

48 Tossols-Basil Athletics Stadium, site plan.

51   Estadio Braga, Portugal, a stadium set into a former rock quarry.

Estadio Municipal de Braga

Another stadium from those years that pushed the architectural ambitions of the type forward was Eduardo Souto de Moura's Estadio Municipal de Braga (2003) in Portugal. Sited in a former quarry, the ground sits in a space carved out from the side of a mountain, with muscular site-cast concrete stands positioned shoulder to shoulder with the face-cut rock. Taking full advantage of the qualities of the site, Souto de Moura's stadium sits in sombre repose, with all the necessary services for game day tucked under the pitch and out of sight. The stands are sheltered by canopy roofs with tensioning cabling crossing the width of the pitch, reminiscent of rope bridges spanning a river. As a whole it is a temple to football designed by an architect at the top of his game, and a project with no real equal anywhere in the world.

(*left*) 52   Estadio Braga, circulation.

Soccer Stadium La Balastera

Not long after Souto de Moura's Estadio Braga was completed, the Soccer Stadium La Balastera (2006) opened in Palencia, Spain. Designed by Francisco Mangado, it sits on the eastern edge of town and the architect had particular urban visions that informed the design, namely that the stadium should offer an iconic identity for the city in which it is located. Following from that was the aim to allow for the stadium to take on a role in the daily civic life of the city. In order to achieve those aims, the stadium is wrapped in offices and other non-sport facilities, with storeys scaled to minimise the often overwhelming mass of a stadium, especially important as this project is close to a residential neighbourhood. The cladding on the public facades, composed of perforated aluminium, serves to further soften the visual impact of the building's mass. Finally, the lighting towers at the four corners, especially when illuminated at night, provide a visual place-maker for the city at large. Though the stadium eschews direct reference to the rich architectural language of a city that dates to the eleventh century, nevertheless it is now widely recognised as what the architect intended, an icon of the city. Indeed, the global recognition that La Balastera has earned is perhaps outsize to what one might expect for a sporting structure in a town of fewer than 100,000 residents.

54   La Balastera, perforated aluminium facade and light tower.

53   La Balastera, Palencia, Spain, circulation ramp with shadow of the stadium's name.

55   La Balastera, compact stands with ample views of the surrounding neighbourhood.

56   La Balastera, a striking stadium scaled
to fit into a small city.

57   La Balastera, the lighting tower at night.

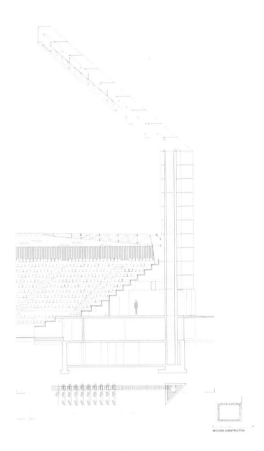

59   La Balastera, section.

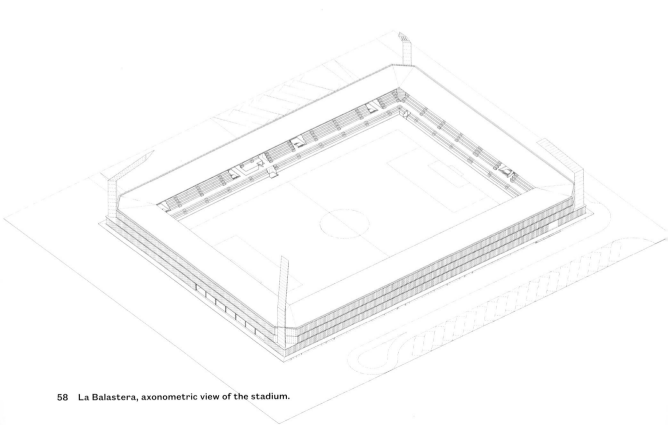

58   La Balastera, axonometric view of the stadium.

University of Phoenix Stadium

Somewhat in contrast to the efforts of Mangado in Palencia, although built at the same time, Peter Eisenman and Populous collaborated on the University of Phoenix Stadium (2006) in the northwestern suburbs of Phoenix, Arizona. The stadium is the home ground of the National Football League team the Arizona Cardinals, but it is named after a for-profit college with over 140,000 students enrolled at 91 satellite campuses across the country and online. The University has no sports teams that play in the stadium, or anywhere else for that matter; it purchased the naming rights in the same fashion as many other corporations do in the United States and around the world. Thus, this project is rather curiously about giving an iconic identity to a faceless corporate entity and its anonymous students and is located in the placeless, anodyne suburbs of a low-density, sprawling city. Surrounded by a veritable sea of surface parking, University of Phoenix is characteristic in its siting and relationship to

its surroundings of so many American suburban stadia. And yet, it has some elements that powerfully differentiate it from its national peers: first, the inclusion of Eisenman (who, although a fan of football, had never worked on a stadium before) on the design team; second, a fully retractable pitch as well as roof, weighing 10,000 and 50,000 US tons respectively; and third, a facade of metal panels and glass that was quite novel for its time. Loosely informed in its shape by native cactus plants common to the area, the stadium's metal-clad curves also call to mind, as Jeffrey Kipnis points out, the architecture of the 14,000 cars parked at the stadium on game day.[24] The suburb in which the stadium sits arose out of the hegemony of the automobile. In a similar fashion, this stadium is shaped by the obligation to accommodate the demands cars place on these types of buildings: a sea of surface parking. The retractable pitch, which slides out into an open-air 'parking spot' of its own, is now regarded as a defining feature of the stadium and is even included in its logo.

60   University of Phoenix Stadium, Arizona, view of the pitch rolled out into its parking space.

61 Ciutadella Park Sports Centre, Barcelona, Spain, the view at night.

62 Ciutadella Park Sports Centre, a timber-wrapped sports centre adjacent to one of Barcelona's major parks.

63 Ciutadella Park Sports Centre, a project scaled to fit into an existing, dense urban setting.

Ciutadella Park Sports Centre

The compact urban site of the Ciutadella Park Sports Centre in Barcelona (Battle i Roig Arquitectes, 2009) is typical of many sport architecture projects, even if the form it takes is not. Not properly a stadium but a multi-sport complex, nevertheless it merits inclusion here for the way in which it resolves the common problems of scale and materiality in a building that abuts much older, established urban forms. Built on a site that includes the remains of the 1714 citadel built by King Felipe V, the project is in one of the most densely populated districts in the city. That density makes finding a site for a complex as large as this challenging, if not impossible in most cases. Seeking to fit in with the surrounding park structures, the building locates a number of its primary amenities below street level, allowing it to maintain the same roofline as the neighbouring buildings. The result is a delicately realised irregular dimensioned box wrapped in wooden slats that both provide sun shading and blend in with the surrounding tree canopy.

Aviva Stadium

A site with similar physical constraints and a long, well-known history is home to the Aviva Stadium in Dublin (Populous, 2010). It is built on the site of the former Lansdowne Road Stadium, which had hosted Irish rugby since 1876. When plans were drawn up for Aviva, it faced a number of hurdles – the brief called for the new 50,000-seat stadium to have a smaller footprint than the 23,000-seat stadium it was replacing. The neighbourhood that the site is located in was by then a densely populated residential area where the houses had rights to light and views, meaning the new stadium would have to grow in seating while shrinking in urban impact. Noise control during matches and events would also need to be managed. An active railway running along the boundary of the site meant that demolition and construction would have to be scheduled to minimise disruption of public transport. There were two major strategies that propelled the success of Aviva. The first was the use of parametric software tools to design

64   Aviva Stadium, Dublin, Ireland, with dynamic curves defining the experience on the interior.

65   Aviva Stadium, the translucent roof is designed to contain crowd noise inside the ground.

the complex curvatures that define the stadium enclosure. These curves enable the building to accommodate the required seating while still nestling into the one-to-two storey residential buildings that surround it, and they serve a secondary function of containing crowd and event noise. The second strategy was to clad the stadium in transparent polycarbonate panels, allowing light to penetrate into the structure. The panels are offset one from the other in order to allow air to move through the concourse spaces, minimising the need for artificial lighting and heating, ventilation and air-conditioning systems. The polycarbonate material changes appearance over the course of the day and in different weather conditions, again helping to minimise the visual mass of the building.

66   Aviva Stadium, from a distance the polycarbonate skin gives the stadium a remarkably lightweight appearance.

(*left*) 67   Aviva Stadium, the curves of the facade also help the stadium settle into its neighbourhood setting.

68   Custoias Football Club, Portugal, a nearly all-white stand, sheltered by a roof resembling a massive gable.

Custoias Football Club

Sensitivity to pre-existing conditions of a site drives decision-making in less dense urban contexts as well. For the Custoias Football Club in Portugal (Guilherme Machado Vaz, 2009), the architect exploited the slope of the site to slot in multiple tiered levels, some of which sit below the pitch, minimising the visual conflict between the terrain and the level playing surface. A strict control over colour palette and material finishes compound the effect of the massing choices, resulting in a plinth-like structure on the main public facade and a wonderfully elegant stand facing the pitch.

69   Custoias Football Club, the stadium is set into a sloping site.

70   Custoias Football Club, the mix of material and colour gives the project a sculptural quality.

London 2012 Olympic Stadium

In 2012 London hosted the city's third Summer Olympic Games, which of course meant the construction of a new Olympic Stadium for the city. In the aftermath of the 2004 Summer Games in Athens, where wildly expensive venues went unused after the closing ceremonies, as well as the cost overruns of New Wembley and the global financial crisis of 2008, the brief for the 2012 Games was 'legacy' and 'embracing the temporary'. Every venue was expected to have a clearly defined legacy use for after the Games, and those that did not would be temporary. The London Olympic Stadium (Populous, 2011) actually was a bit of both – a stadium designed to accommodate track and field sports and 80,000 spectators that after the Games would be downsized to a venue roughly half that size that would become the home ground of one of the many London-based football clubs. In Olympics mode, the stadium was defined by the triangular geometries of the structural steel system that wrapped the ground, the roof truss ringing the seating bowl and the monumental lighting towers that rose above the roofline. In contrast to the 2008 Olympic Stadium in Beijing – massive, heavy, expensive, sculptural and extravagant in its use of concrete – the London Stadium was lightweight, giving the appearance of being fully demountable and modifiable. After the Games, many of the temporary venues disappeared and significant development of housing, shopping and commercial venues radically transformed the character of this part of East London.[25]

71   London 2012 Olympic Stadium, pictured here after the Games, in preparation for conversion to its legacy use as the home of West Ham United Football Club; note the defining triangular light towers.

(*above*) 72   London Olympic Stadium, Stratford, East London, in the midst of conversion to its legacy use; the lighting towers now inverted from the new, much larger roof.

In legacy mode, after a protracted legal battle involving a number of clubs and the City of London, the Olympic Stadium underwent a transformation to become the home of West Ham United Football Club. That transformation, also led by Populous and completed in 2016, involved the construction of a new roof to shelter the 57,000 spectators for the football ground. This meant the removal of the existing steel roof system and iconic lighting towers, which were replaced with a cable-net roof structure covering 45,000 square metres – the largest of its kind in the world. The towers now hang under the roof, helping to define the character of the interior space.

(*right*) 73   London Olympic Stadium, an anchor in an increasingly redeveloped area of East London.

74 Tele2 Arena, Stockholm, Sweden, shows how unconventional massing was needed to fit the stadium into a compact urban site.

75 Tele2 Arena, a wrap of perforated metal frames views out into the city.

76   Tele2 Arena, massive trusses define the feel of the interior.

Tele2 Arena

The Tele2 Arena in Stockholm opened in 2013, not long after the London Olympic Stadium, and it also sought to link inventive sport architecture with long-term urban development. Designed by White Arkitekter, the brief for the multi-purpose stadium called for 30,000 spectators in football mode and 45,000 in concert mode. The problem was that the site chosen for the stadium was too small to accommodate that many spectators using conventional stadium design and construction methods. The client also wanted a project of formal significance and scale, one that would attract international attention, further complicating the brief. The solution came in the form of split-tier geometry for the seating bowl, with the lower tier more conventional and symmetrical and the upper tier asymmetrical and wider than the lower tier. This gives the stadium a basket-like form and, set as it is on a plinth to

77   Tele2 Arena, the metal panels are arrayed in a weave pattern.

78   Tele2 Arena, at night the stadium lights up, marking the neighbourhood.

79   Tele2 Arena, although undeniably large, does not overwhelm the pedestrian plaza adjacent to it.

allow for street traffic to flow underneath, gives it the monumental quality sought by the clients. The building is wrapped by a perforated metal facade that allows simultaneous views into and out of the stadium, helping to link it to the surrounding neighbourhood in everyday life.

Levi's Stadium

A number of American football teams built new facilities in the second decade of the twenty-first century, and these projects foreshadowed an arms race between clubs to build the newest and most advanced stadium. And since stadia in the USA are often substantially subsidised by public funds, this meant that the competition was also between cities to hold onto teams by funnelling tax dollars to these ambitious stadia projects. Setting aside

the reality that public funding of private revenue-generating enterprises owned by a small cohort of billionaires is terrible public policy, many of these projects did at least possess some admirable formal qualities. Among these is the new home of the San Francisco 49ers, Levi's Stadium (HNTB, 2014), named in the American tradition after a company, in this case a denim vendor, rather than the team or site. Located in Santa Clara, just over 40 miles from the city of the team's name, Levi's is part of an emerging trend in stadia design emphasising sustainability. Levi's aim to be the first net-zero electricity stadium in the world was enabled via extensive photovoltaic arrays, water reclamation systems and geothermal energy-saving systems. The building was awarded a Leadership in Energy and Environmental Design (LEED) Gold rating

(rare for stadia). Formally, the defining element of the project is the two grand stairs that spectators climb to get to the seating areas. These are located on either side of the 'face' of the stadium, a tower with shops at street level and the suites and press box above.

US Bank Stadium

In Minneapolis, the Minnesota Vikings opened their new home field, US Bank (HKS), in 2016, replacing the Hubert H. Humphrey Dome. That structure, opened in 1982, was named after a former senator, vice president and one-time presidential candidate from Minnesota. The new stadium takes some of its visual cues from the nearby Guthrie Theater designed by Jean Nouvel and completed in 2006. The stadium is angular and asymmetrical, and it makes significant use of ETFE on the roof and glazed walls along the western elevations to allow for interior views of the city skyline and ample natural illumination. The choice of transparent roof and wall surfaces was driven by the cold and harsh climate of Minneapolis, which

make a retractable roof (now considered standard for National Football League stadia) suboptimal. On game days when the climate is amenable to open-air conditions, the world's largest doors can be opened to achieve an effect akin to an open, retractable-roofed stadium.

Mercedes-Benz Stadium

In Atlanta, the Falcons were also moving out of their former home, the Georgia Dome. Opened in just 1992, the decision in 2010 to vacate points to another trend related to stadia in the United States: their ever-decreasing lifespan. The Dome was not widely admired as a design object, it is safe to say, but most fans regarded it as a perfectly comfortable place to take in a game. Built at a cost of around $215 million, its replacement, the Mercedes-Benz Stadium (HOK, 2017), would run to $1.6 billion. Much of that cost is associated with novel structural elements like the eight-panel ETFE-clad retractable roof, known as 'the oculus', and the advanced technologies meant to add to the spectacle of game day such as the 'halo', the world's

(*top left*) 80   Levi's Stadium, Santa Clara, California, although as relentlessly branded as any American stadium today, also offers a novel, apartment block-like facade.

(*bottom left*) 81   Levi's Stadium, one of the two pleasantly thin grand stairs that flank the main facade.

(*above*) 82   US Bank Stadium, Minneapolis, home to the Minnesota Vikings, designed to echo a ship, and fully enclosed with walls of glass and an ETFE roof.

83   Mercedes-Benz Stadium, Atlanta, Georgia, the replacement for the just 25-year-old Georgia Dome to the left, is defined by its faceted walls along the facade and its eight-panel retractable roof.

84 BBVA Compass Stadium, Houston, Texas, a single-sport stadium built for football, still a relative rarity in the United States.

85 BBVA Compass Stadium, clad in a framework of grey and brightly coloured metal mesh, is meant to evoke the atmosphere of more established European grounds.

first 360-degree LED video display. As in Levi's, the designers emphasised sustainability as a defining feature of the stadium, which was the first in the United States, and only the second in the world, to be awarded LEED Platinum status, the highest ranking available.

BBVA Compass Stadium

Managers of Major League Soccer teams in the USA also understood the economic advantages and publicity that a new stadium could garner, and many became clients for novel urban projects. The most notable of these in recent years is the BBVA Compass Stadium (Populous, 2012) in Houston, Texas – home to the Houston Dynamo. This soccer-specific stadium differs from its National Football League counterparts in many interesting ways. Although many new NFL stadia are multi-purpose, the BBVA is designed for a single sport, seats about a third of what a new NFL ground would and, at $95 million, cost a fraction of a new American football venue. Populous brought in Chris Lee, who was the lead on the Emirates Stadium in London, to work on BBVA with the aspiration of crafting an authentic soccer venue in the American context. The modest budget meant that material choices on this project would differ from the NFL. Instead of ETFE, the facade of the BBVA is metal mesh set in triangular frames and orange polycarbonate-clad spaces at the pedestrian level. During the day, the stadium has a vibrant quality, very much defined by bright colours and metallic shine. At night, the mesh disappears and the stadium glows.

Redeveloping older stadia

Eisstadion Inzell

Some of the more architecturally ambitious projects of this era were renovations and upgrades rather than outright new projects. In Inzell, Germany, Behnisch Architekten + Pohl Architekten took a speed skating arena from the mid-1960s and updated it dramatically with a high-performance intelligent roof structure. Designed to provide

86   Eisstadion Inzell, Germany, an arena from the 1960s, gets updated with a high-performance roof.

87   Eisstadion Inzell, a system of 17 skylights is fitted into the tensile fabric roof.

88   Eisstadion Inzell, a facade of glass wrapping
the building provides views of the nearby Bavarian
mountains.

89　Eisstadion Inzell blends in with its snow-covered surroundings in the winter.

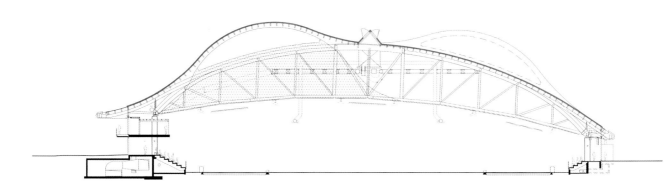

Speed Skating Stadium
Cross Section
Inzell, Germany

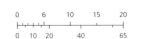

90　Eisstadion Inzell, a monumental truss allows for a column-free interior.

ample natural light via 17 north-facing skylights, the roof system also provides thermal control by redirecting cool air back down towards the ice. From the exterior, the roof gives the impression of snow-covered slopes in brilliant white. On the interior of the wide-span structure there are no columns to obstruct views through the continuous glass facade of the nearby Bavarian Alps.

Maracana Stadium

Another project from the mid-century era that received an upgrade via a new roofing system is Rio de Janeiro's iconic Maracana Stadium. Ahead of the 2014 World Cup, the seating bowl was upgraded, moving to a single-tiered system, and the concrete roof demolished and replaced by Schlaich Bergermann Partner with a lightweight tensioned fibreglass canopy coated in luminescent white PTFE. The new roof covers nearly 95 per cent of the

91   Maracana Stadium, Rio de Janeiro, Brazil, upgraded for the 2014 World Cup.

92   Maracana Stadium, showing the completed new roof.

93   Maracana Stadium, showing the roof, a lightweight tensioned fibreglass canopy, under construction.

94   Los Angeles Memorial Coliseum, California, named, and on the exterior clearly modelled after, the Coliseum. This collegiate venue is in the midst of extensive renovations, the first of which was a modern double tier of luxury suites towering above the seating bowl.

seating area. PTFE, or Polytetrafluoroethylene, is an extremely weather-resistant material with very low friction properties. These characteristics make it a good choice for roofing conditions that are difficult to access or clean regularly.

Los Angeles Memorial Coliseum

In equally sunny Los Angeles, the University of California's stadium, the Los Angeles Memorial Coliseum (John and Donald Parkinson, 1923), was upgraded with a new suite of boxes built atop the

older concrete bowl beneath. An elegant curved box of glass and metal, it cantilevers over the bowl below and is a powerful reminder that additions and upgrades can dramatically revise a structure.

Estadio Municipal de Pasaron

In Pontevedra, Spain, another older venue was also transformed – the Estadio Municipal de Pasaron, which opened in 1965. Starting in 2006, a six-year transformation by IDOM Architects aimed to revitalise both the stadium and its

95 Estadio Municipal de Pasaron, Pontevedra, Spain, an 11,000-seat ground with outsize formal ambitions.

96 Estadio Municipal de Pasaron, the stadium fits into its surroundings, with only the light towers rising above neighbouring structures to serve as calling cards for the ground.

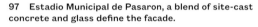

97   Estadio Municipal de Pasaron, a blend of site-cast concrete and glass define the facade.

98   Estadio Municipal de Pasaron, at one corner the enclosing walls pull back and a capacious stair draws spectators in.

99   Estadio Municipal de Pasaron, the handling of concrete is a defining element of the design throughout the ground.

100 Estadio Municipal de Pasaron, showing apertures cut through the concrete in an asymmetrical array.

101 Estadio Municipal de Pasaron, the concrete is not hidden away behind some other finished material but is celebrated instead for its sculptural qualities.

102 Estadio Municipal de Pasaron, site plan showing the relation of the stadium to the surrounding town.

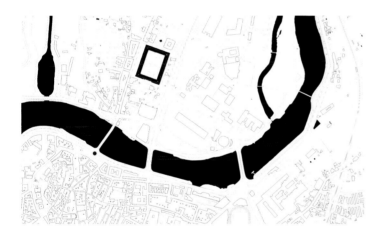

103 Estadio Municipal de Pasaron, section cut of the new stand.

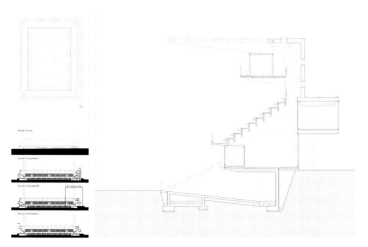

surrounding neighbourhood, which the architects diplomatically describe as 'untidy'.[26] New stands, a new roof and, critically, a new circulation system inside and around the ground all enabled the generation of a new city square and park around the stadium. The amenities tucked into the base of the stands can be accessed both from the inside and outside of the ground, giving the stadium a more engaged day-to-day presence in the neighbourhood. The structural systems are executed primarily in site-cast concrete, with circular perforations arrayed in a seemingly random fashion in the exterior walls and generous cantilevered overhanging projections providing a

defining urban character to the building. Lighting towers scaled nearly twice the height of the top of the stands and positioned at the four corners give this 11,000-seat stadium a powerful presence in the skyline of a city of 83,000.

San Mames

Clients and even most fans generally regard a new stadium as an unalloyed positive development in the life of a club. But the reality is that new stadia come with a range of complications all their own – the loss of identity, the threat to a robust game-day atmosphere, a trading in of heritage for revenue. Therefore clubs, especially those with a

104   New San Mames, Bilbao, Spain, 'the Cathedral', at night.

105 New San Mames, 480 white ETFE cushions clad the exterior.

106 New San Mames features red, one of the club's colours, throughout the stadium.

107 New San Mames, the tensile roof.

well-established culture and identity, face a host of challenges that the design of a new stadium has to address. Such was the case in Bilbao, where construction for a new stadium broke ground in 2010. That venue, the 'New' San Mames, was the replacement for the 'Old' San Mames, built in 1913, and famous as a stadium with one of the most intense game-day atmospheres in Europe. The significance of the stadium in the life of the city and its residents is hinted at in its nickname, 'La Catedral'.

108   New San Mames, detail of the ETFE cushions.

109   New San Mames, the tightly disposed seating bowl is designed to maximise atmosphere on game day.

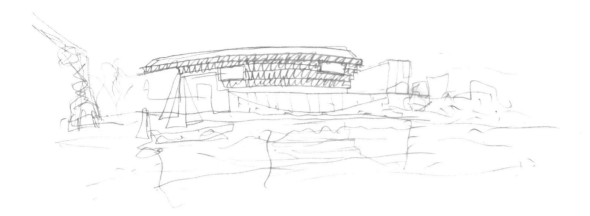

110   New San Mames, early design sketch.

111   New San Mames, site plan.

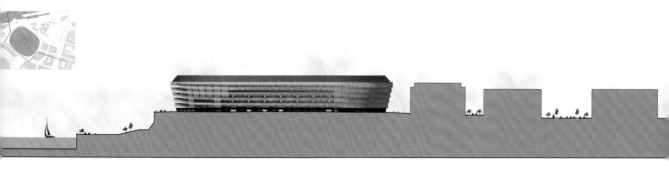

112   New San Mames, showing the massing of the San Mames in relation to neighbouring buildings.

IDOM Architects understood the challenge that replacing the San Mames entailed, noting that they aimed to design a building that 'must be introduced categorically and with force'.[27] This sensibility guided both the organisation and design of the interior and exterior space. On the interior, the stands are designed and placed to maximise crowd noise and pitched to give the away team the impression of being surrounded at close range by a hostile crowd. On the exterior the facade deploys an array of ETFE pillows twisted into a range of deformed rectangles. Illuminated at night, it serves as a symbol of the city and its home club.

Stade Jean Bouin

Several older venues have been upgraded via recladding, a strategy that often yields mixed results, but when done well can be particularly striking. Perhaps the best recent examples of this approach to updating stadia are to be found in Paris, Marseille and Johannesburg. The Stade Jean Bouin in Paris is a rugby ground that dates to 1925 and is located in close quarters with two other icons of sport in Paris – Roland Garros, home of the French Open, and the Parc des Princes (Roger Taillibert, 1972), home of Paris Saint-Germain Football Club. All of these sporting spaces are located in the 16th arrondissement, which is one of the most affluent neighbourhoods in the city. This historic setting is also home to museums, the Bois de Boulogne (the second largest public park in the city) and residences of many of France's economic, political and cultural elite. Indeed, the Jean Bouin sits across the street from Le Corbusier's studio apartment in the top two floors of the Molitor Building. Designed between 1931 and 1934, Le Corbusier lived there for over 30 years until his death in 1965.

In 2010 the decision was made to upgrade the stadium, enlarging it to 20,000 seats as well as adding a gymnasium, underground parking, and office and broadcasting spaces. Completed in 2013, this necessitated a nearly complete rebuilding of Jean Bouin, with the most striking features including a new facade and roof for the stadium. Its location meant that the appearance of the building would be as important as its performance. The architect for the project, Rudy Ricciotti, recognised this from the outset, commenting that a primary aim was to avoid 'a violent impact on the urban landscape'.[28] Two major moves were critical for this to happen. First, a number of operations and the parking were sunk in the three below-ground levels, which keeps the stadium from overwhelming its neighbours. The second was the choice to clad the stadium in ultra-high performance concrete (UHPC), a favourite material of Ricciotti throughout his career. As the building

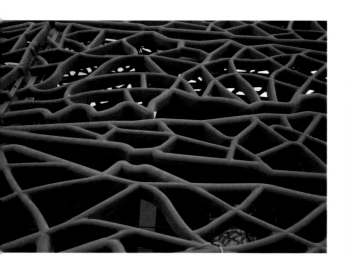
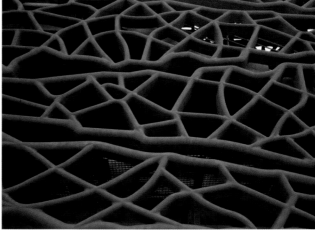

113 & 114   Stade Jean Bouin, Paris, France, details of the triangular pre-cast concrete panels cladding the stadium.

115   Stade Jean Bouin is adjacent to the neo-brutalist Parc des Princes (Roger Taillibert, 1972).

identity for the stadium and club. SCAU chose an undulating metal frame for the roof structure, with a PTFE fabric stretched over it. The PTFE also turns and runs down the sides of the stadium, in a voluptuous curve that means the roof at one end of the ground is higher than the other (somewhat reminiscent of the Aviva Stadium in Dublin). The material is milky white and translucent, and the roof itself is scalloped, giving the stadium elevations something of the quality of a giant seashell – appropriate for its coastal location. Finally, as in the Stade Jean Bouin, the form of the roof holds sound inside the ground, enlivening the game-day atmosphere. At night, when the stadium is illuminated from the interior, it is transformed

envelope is undulating and asymmetrical, the cladding is composed of 3,600 triangular panels of pre-cast UHPC, each roughly 9 metres by 2.5 metres and 4.5 centimetres thick. A less complex concrete panel system in the roof allows for the insertion of light-diffusing glass to shelter the spectators below from rain and harsh light. The asymmetrical form of the envelope not only provides formal tension and visual play as one circulates the stadium, but also is designed to prevent excess crowd noise from escaping the ground, making the game-day experience a spectacle while keeping neighbours from experiencing undue crowd disturbance.

Stade Velodrome

A second project, also in France, that deploys an elegant cladding system to upgrade an older stadium is the Stade Velodrome in Marseille. Built in 1937, the Stade Velodrome hosted football, rugby and, for a time, cycling, hence its name. In 2014, the club increased seating at the ground to 67,000 along with other improvements in order to host the 2016 European Championship semi-final. SCAU were chosen to design a new roof and enclosure for the renovated stadium, one that would shelter fans as well as providing a stronger sense of visual

116   Stade Velodrome, Marseille, France, detail of the exterior and the PTFE fabric roof.

117　Stade Velodrome, interior view of the sweeping roof structure framing the mountains in the distance.

118 Stade Vélodrome, the curving roof structure offers multiple elevations to the project depending on which direction one approaches it from.

119   Stade Velodrome, the crisp, scalloped white roof.

120   Stade Velodrome, the spectacular roof wraps the stadium, at one point swooping down to touch the ground.

121   FNB Stadium, Johannesburg, South Africa, often called 'Soccer City', a stadium clad in multi-coloured terracotta tiles.

into a glowing icon in the city skyline, as noticeable as any skyscraper.

FNB Stadium

The redevelopment project in Johannesburg, South Africa, was also driven by the demands of hosting an international football tournament, in this case the 2010 Fédération Internationale de Football Association (FIFA) World Cup. The FNB Stadium opened in 1989, with a capacity of 80,000. For the World Cup it was upgraded to over 90,000, making it the largest stadium in Africa. Although scale alone can, and often does, suffice as the iconic quality pursued by both clients and architects, for the FNB and the World Cup, which was intended to introduce a modern, democratic and prosperous post-Apartheid South Africa to the world, something more was required. Populous chose to model the redeveloped stadium after the African calabash, a gourd often hollowed out to make into a cooking utensil or food container. In order to accomplish this, the stadium is clad with terracotta tiles in a range of reds and earth tones, set in a mosaic pattern and punched through with glazed apertures in a seemingly random (though not to say chaotic) fashion. At night, lighting installed at the base of the exterior cladding lights up and, in the words of the designers, gives the impression of fire underneath a cooking pot. The roof system is, like the Stade Velodrome, a metal frame with PTFE fabric, here coloured to resemble the surrounding landscape. The seating is arrayed in ten tiers, nine of which are aligned, according to the architects, 'geographically with the nine other stadia used in South Africa 2010 . . . with an additional tenth line that aims towards Berlin's Olympic Stadium'.[29] Although formally named FNB for sponsorship purposes, the stadium is also colloquially known as 'the Calabash' and 'Soccer City' (a reflection of its scale). In the years since the World Cup, the FNB has hosted a number of major concerts and sporting events.

Small-scale stadia projects

Stadium du Littoral

Several modestly sized projects in unexpected places generated outcomes that are well worth mentioning. The Stadium du Littoral (OLGGA Architects, 2011) in the commune of Grande-Synthe in northern France (population less than

122   Stadium du Littoral, Grande-Synthe, France, view out to the pitch through the transparent mesh wall and ceiling enclosure.

123   Stadium du Littoral, showing the modestly scaled stand, divided into two parts via a central aperture.

124   Stadium du Littoral, exterior stair and bridge leading into the stand.

125 Stadium du Littoral, asymmetrical pattern of rectangles cut into the street level wall around the outside of the ground.

126 Stadium du Littoral at sunset.

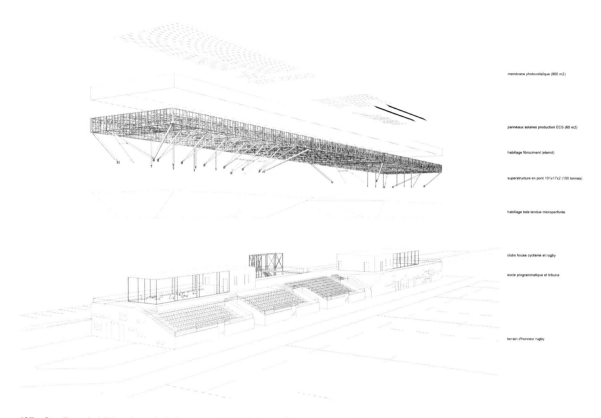

membrane photovoltaïque (800 m2)

panneaux solaires production ECS (60 m2)

habillage fibrociment (eternit)

superstructure en pont 101x17x2 (100 tonnes)

habillage toile tendue microperforée

clubs house cyclisme et rugby

socle programmatique et tribune

terrain d'honneur rugby

127   Stadium du Littoral, exploded axonometric of the roof structure and cladding.

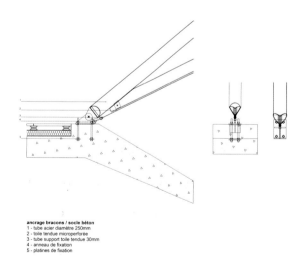

ancrage bracons / socle béton
1 - tube acier diamétre 250mm
2 - toile tendue microperforée
3 - tube support toile tendue 30mm
4 - anneau de fixation
5 - platines de fixation

128   Stadium du Littoral, detail of the anchoring
system for the roof.

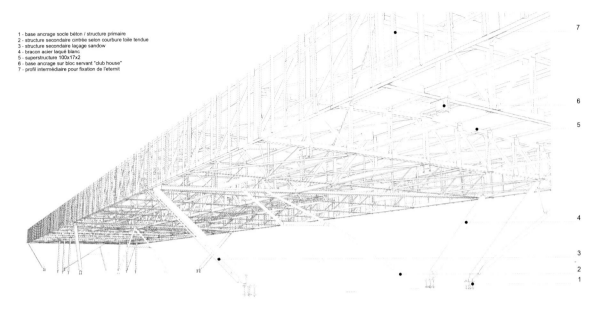

1 - base ancrage socle béton / structure primaire
2 - structure secondaire cintrée selon courbure toile tendue
3 - structure secondaire laçage sandow
4 - bracon acier laqué blanc
5 - superstructure 100x17x2
6 - base ancrage sur bloc servant "club house"
7 - profil intermédiaire pour fixation de l'eternit

7

6

5

4

3

2

1

129   Stadium du Littoral, detail of the roof structure.

24,000) has seating for just 671 spectators, but accommodates them with an élan that eludes many larger and more expensive projects. The brief for the project is multi-sport, as the du Littoral serves as a community athletics centre for some 4,000 resident members. The twelve-hectare complex includes three rugby and two football fields, a running track, an archery round, two clubhouses, locker rooms, a community recreation room and administrative offices. Situated alongside the major roadway leading into the Grande-Synthe, it offers an updated, modern visual identity for the town. The massing of the stands from a distance gives the appearance of a parallelogram floating above the green of the pitch. Sections of the mass are carved out to allow for the insertion of seating and other visitor spaces. A restrained, nearly uniform colour palette is used across the range of materials sheltering the seating, minimising an emphasis on individual structural elements. Inside the stadium, a micro-perforated stretch-mounted fabric covers many of the interior spaces. This shields views of the structural system and gives the building a lightweight and elegant air. The stadium is built to meet France's 2005 THPE (very high energy performance) building standards, with heat pumps, 700 square metres of photovoltaic panels on the roof, and another 40 square metres of photovoltaic panels that provide 50 per cent of the hot water used at the facility.

Plaine des Sports

A second project also by OLGGA Architect, the Plaine des Sports in Saint-Paul-les-Dax (population 10,000), deploys a similar strategy for an athletics complex with programming similar to the du Littoral, here with seating for 500. Again located alongside the major vehicular access to the town, this project also has to negotiate the presence of several protected species of birds and butterflies, wetland and a nearby stream, all of which had to be preserved. Although modest in scale compared to many urban stadia projects, these two stadia are reminders that sustainability – both as an ecological and social imperative – can usefully inform elegant and socially engaged projects.

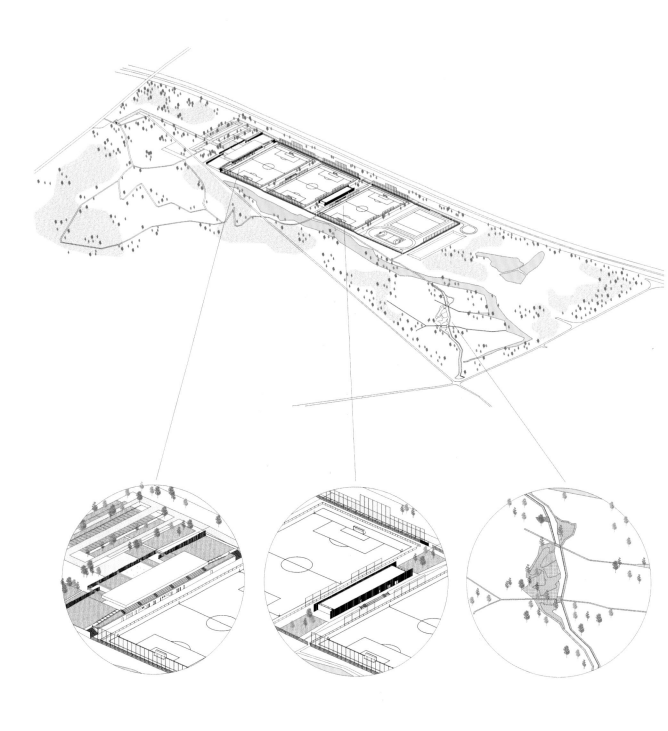

130   Plaine des Sports, Saint-Paul-les-Dax, France,
site plan and details.

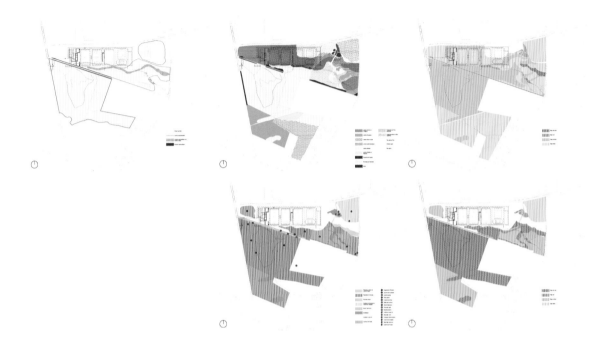

131   Plaine des Sports, mapping the ecological conditions with which the project had to negotiate.

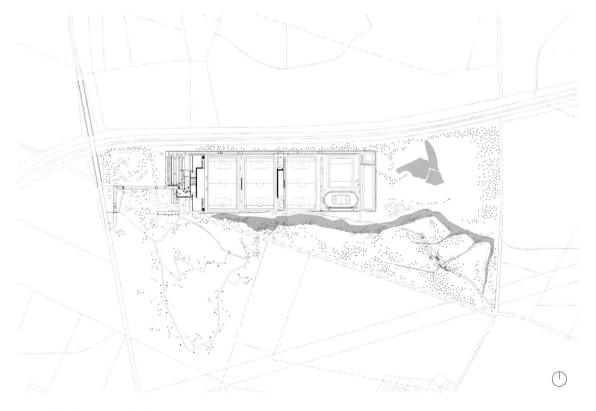

132   Plaine des Sports, site plan.

133 Plaine des Sports, wood bridge and footpath elevated above the protected landscape.

134 Plaine des Sports, the path to the stadium and pitches.

135   Plaine des Sports, aerial view of the stadium at sunset.

136   Plaine des Sports, entrance to the ground with wooden post fencing.

137 Plaine des Sports, seating area with club
amenities behind a glass wall.

138   Plaine des Sports, the bar area.

139   Plaine des Sports, the view of the stands from the pitch.

140   Borisov Arena, Barysaw, Belarus, is situated among a stand of pines.

Borisov Arena

In Barysaw, Belarus, OFIS Architects designed an arena for 13,000 that opened in 2014 and is one of the most exciting stadium projects of the last 20 years. A striking, shimmering orb set within a stand of tall pines, Borisov Arena looks like something from another time and place. Amoeba-like shapes cut into the metal skin tightly wrapped around the structure of the stadium offer glimpses into the shops and walkways contained between the skin and the stands. During the day the stadium is a shiny visitor from some futuristic footballing planet, while at night it takes on a glow as if it could lift off at any moment. That something this delicate and idiosyncratic is the home ground for a football team whose name

141   Borisov Arena, detail of the metal skin wrapping the building, with amoeba-shaped openings cut into it.

142   Borisov Arena, formally ambitious without being bombastic, fits well into the daily life of the city.

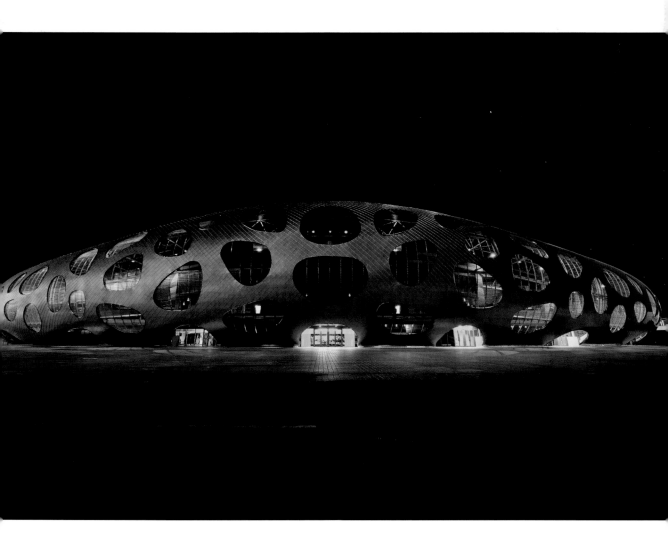

143   Borisov Arena glowing at night like a spaceship.

145   Borisov Arena, light effects on the interior generated by the apertures.

146   Borisov Arena, view of the pitch.

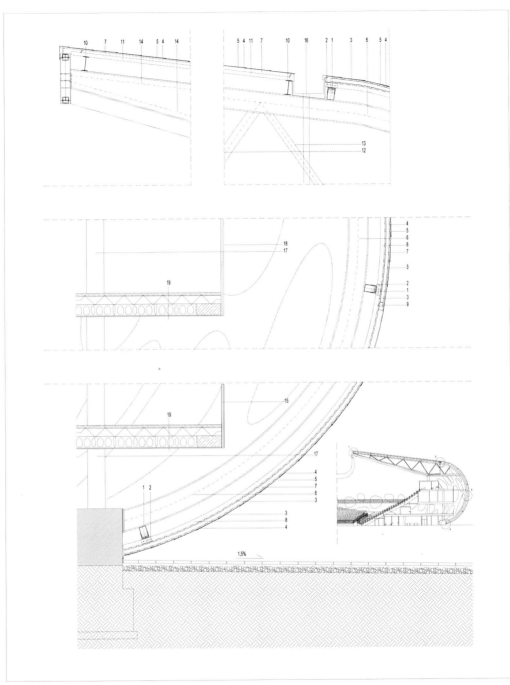

1. TUBE, 300/200/6 mm
2. TUBE, 140/80/8 mm
3. ALUMINUM TRAPEZE, E35/207/1,5 mm
4. SEPARATION LAYER, d = 2 mm
5. ALUMINUM SHEET
7. Z PROFILE, 3 mm, STEEL
8. TUBE 120/60/4 mm

9. U PROFILE, 3mm
10. IPE 400
11. TRAPEZOIDAL SHEET
12. HEB 300
13. HEB 200
14. HEB 360
15. FENCE, EXPANDED METAL MESH PANEL

16. WATER DRENAGE
17. CONCRETE COLUMN
18. STRUCTURAL GLASS
19. FLOOR: polished concrete, thermal
insulation, hydro insulation, reinforced metal
slab

147 Borisov Arena, sections.

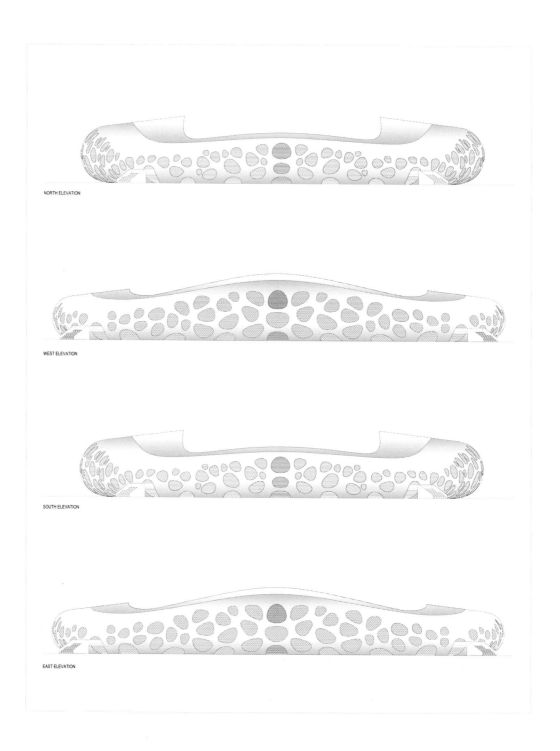

NORTH ELEVATION

WEST ELEVATION

SOUTH ELEVATION

EAST ELEVATION

0   20   40m

148   Borisov Arena, elevations.

149   Ring Stadium, Maribor, Slovenia, in its setting in Slovenia's second largest city.

references the club's origins in Belarus' tractor and automobile industry is especially delightful.

Ring Stadium

OFIS Architects were also responsible for the Ring Stadium in Maribor, Slovenia (2008), where the brief called for the conversion of an existing football pitch with a single stand into a complete stadium with shops, restaurants, swimming pools, a fitness centre and seating for 12,500. Undulating site-cast concrete stands carry the new covered seating areas and provide the stadium with its visual identity.

150   Ring Stadium, the undulating new stands at night.

151 Ring Stadium, the joint where the new stands meet the older, existing stand to the right.

152 Ring Stadium, the view at street level.

153　Ring Stadium, showing glazing wrapping the concourse, allowing for views into the spectacle inside the ground.

154　Ring Stadium, interior, with a translucent new roof sheltering the seats and curving down to meet the older stand at the rear.

NORTH

EAST

ELEVATIONS

155 Ring Stadium, two elevations.

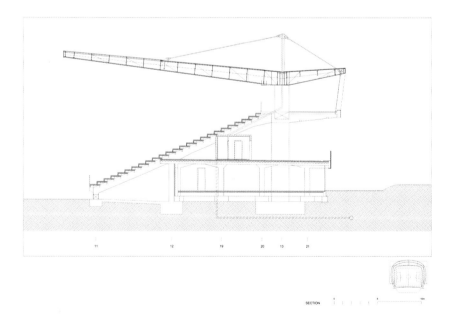

SECTION

156 Ring Stadium, section of the new stand.

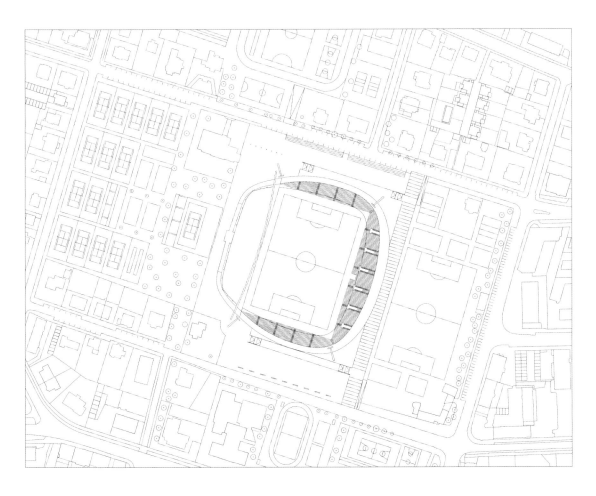

SITEPLAN

0   30   60m

157   Ring Stadium, site plan.

158 Pancho Arena, Felcsut, Hungary, from a distance resembles a
sort of elongated country church more than a football ground.

159   Pancho Arena north facade is dominated by copper, tile and timber, atypical stadium building materials.

Pancho Arena

Another small project, this one in Hungary, likewise uses a highly gestural architectural language to give shape to a ground whose modest scale is no constraint on architectural ambition. The Pancho Arena, designed by Tamas Dobrosi + Doparum Architects, seats just under 4,000, but has an appearance that suggests a level of aesthetic ambition as pronounced as any 60,000+ ground. Copper, timber and concrete are deployed inventively throughout the stadium. The result is a project that from a distance hardly resembles a bowl or stand stadium, looking instead much more like a church. On the interior, a wooden lattice structure is revealed that holds up the roof and itself springs from massive site-cast concrete bases

160   Pancho Arena, with copper domes set atop art nouveau timber elements, and themselves topped by conical spires, again calls to mind some form of ecclesiastical architecture.

161   Pancho Arena, on the interior a timber lattice work springs from concrete bases.

Pancho Arena, Felcsút, Hungary

Cross section - Legend:
1.   Team dressing rooms, press conference room
2.   Press stands, studios, commentary positions
3.   VIP lounge
4.   Skyboxes
5.   Camera positions
6.   Academy dressing rooms
7.   Public facilities (food, beverages, toilets, first ai

0   10   20 m

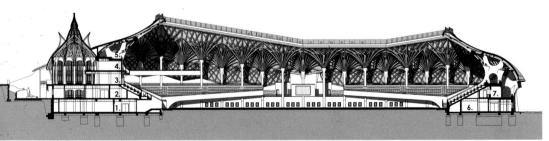

162   Pancho Arena, section.

Pancho Arena, Felcsút, Hungary
North elevation

0   10   20 m

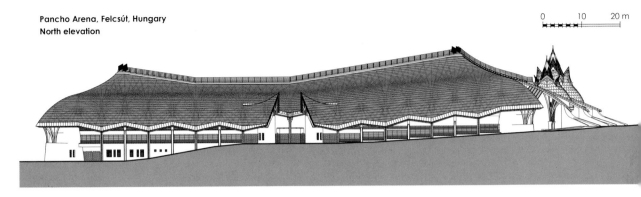

163   Pancho Arena, north elevation.

that also serve as archways to organise circulation around the stands. Formally audacious, the main reservations one might have with the ground have to do with the political ambitions of its sponsor, Hungarian politician Viktor Orban. Orban has a long and, to put it charitably, colourful history on the right wing of Hungarian politics. He has long deployed sport as part of his political agenda, and the Pancho Arena, named after the famous 'Mighty Magyar' Ferenc Puskas, is no different.[30] It remains, nevertheless, an amazing project from a formal perspective.

Pancho Arena, Felcsút, Hungary - Site plan

0   50   100 m

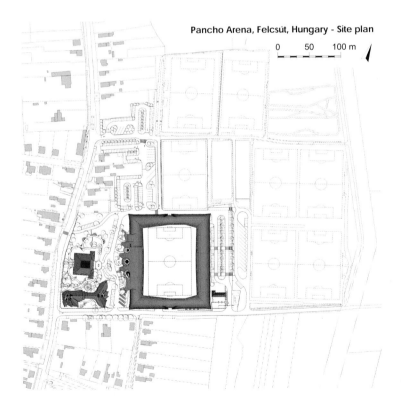

164   Pancho Arena, site plan.

165   Tondiraba Ice Arena, Tallinn, Estonia, is set between a green space and a Soviet-era neighbourhood
of mid high-rise apartment blocks.

166   Tondiraba Ice Arena is defined by simple geometries; a set of concrete rectangular volumes,
with a rectangular void serving as the central entrance.

Tondiraba Ice Arena

Eastern and Central Europe in the second decade of the twenty-first century punched above their weight, with a number of innovative and exciting stadia projects. In Estonia, the Tondiraba Ice Arena in Tallinn (Kadarik Tüür Arhitektid, 2014), built in an effort to revitalise a Soviet-era residential neighbourhood, is a project that exploits the textural qualities of concrete. The success of the arena has much to do with two key moves that the building makes: first, the use of rectangles of varying scales as the organising geometry behind the massing of the project; and second, the light touch of the fenestration patterns that organise the elevations, allowing a project of substantial scale to fit into its surroundings. This project, which is emphatically pragmatic in so many ways, never looks pragmatic. Instead it gives the impression of absolute

167   Tondiraba Ice Arena, the fenestration is likewise all rectangles, organised in a pattern inspired by ice crystals.

intentionality, with every effort made to realise a very large project in a rather inhospitable setting with as much elegance and grace as possible.

168   Tondiraba Ice Arena aimed to spur the revitalisation of the neighbourhood.

169   Tondiraba Ice Arena, detail of the fenestration.

(*right*) 170   Tondiraba Ice Arena, showing the pattern of
the fenestration repeated in the low boundary walls around
the arena.

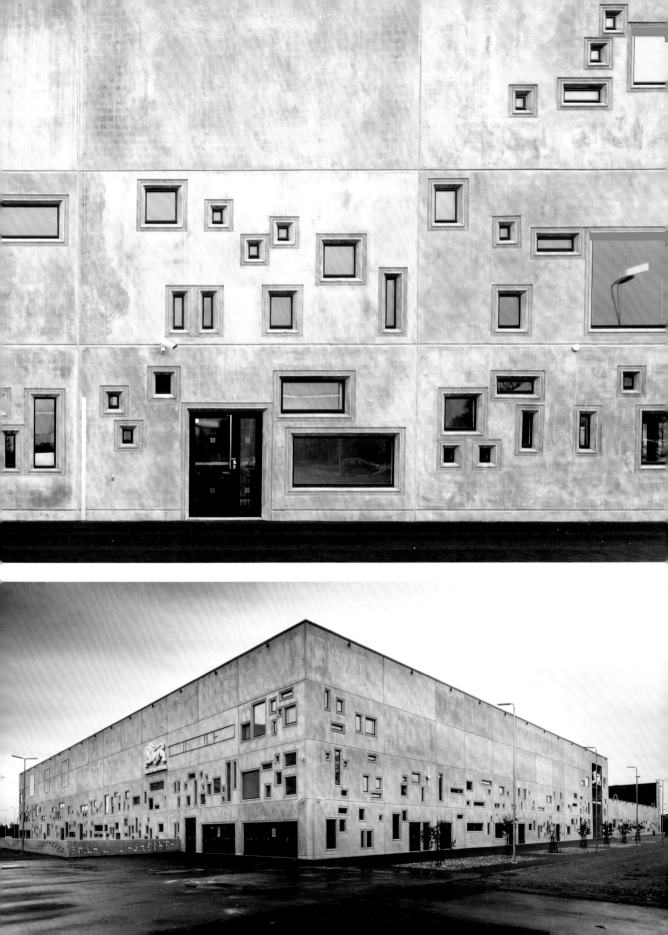

Parnu Stadium

A second project in Estonia also highlights that lofty architectural ambitions are not limited to the grand capital cities of Western Europe. The Parnu Stadium (KAMP Arhitektid, 2016) is a marvel of clean, crisp lines in concrete and wood that seems at once completely modern but pleasingly classical in proportion. Where stadia are often imagined as heavy, massive projects, Parnu is sharply detailed, light on its feet, with a nearly 1:10 plan generating a slender form, and looks as refreshing as the nearby sea. The mix of wood and concrete succeeds because both are detailed to highlight their respective material qualities.

171 Parnu Stadium, Parnu, Estonia, entrance, with concrete panels and wood cladding where the building is cut away to allow ingress.

172 Parnu Stadium, the regular bays that define the public facade.

173　Parnu Stadium at night, with the cantilevered roof of the stand dramatically lit.

174　Parnu Stadium, the view from the stands.

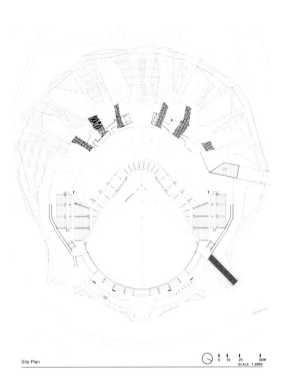

Sonora Stadium

In Mexico in the past decade several stadium projects have stepped out of the concrete bowl tradition that was common there for much of the twentieth century. The Sonora Stadium (3Arquitectura, 2013) in Hermosillo, designed for baseball, sits in view of nearby mountains and is defined by a single, graceful enveloping form. Rust-coloured and set into the arid landscape, the stadium is the visual and physical anchor for the development of a new urban neighbourhood.

(*left*) 175   Sonora Stadium, site plan.

Site Plan

SCALE 1:2000

(*below*) 176   Sonora Stadium, Hermosillo, Mexico, aerial view, with the mountains that inspired the roof line in the distance.

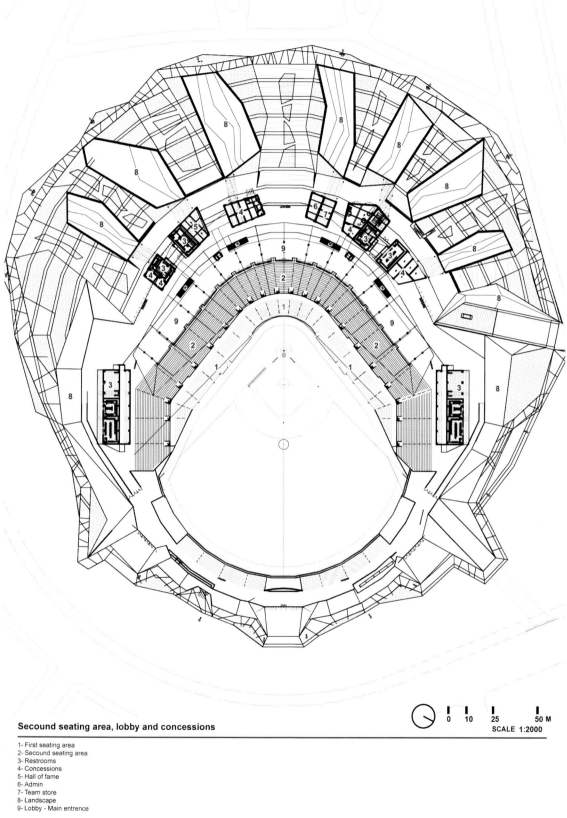

Secound seating area, lobby and concessions

1- First seating area
2- Secound seating area
3- Restrooms
4- Concessions
5- Hall of fame
6- Admin
7- Team store
8- Landscape
9- Lobby - Main entrence

0   10   25   50 M
SCALE 1:2000

177 Sonora Stadium resembles a shell in plan.

178   Sonora Stadium, the view from the field.

179   Sonora Stadium, night-time view during play.

180   Sonora Stadium, a view of the rust-coloured roof whose form echoes the mountains behind it.

181   Sonora Stadium, the landscape around the ground is populated with native plantings.

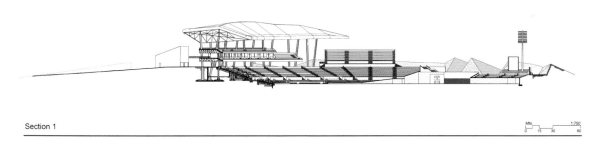

Section 1

Mts   1:750
0   15   30   60

182   Sonora Stadium, section.

183   BBVA Bancomer Stadium, Guadalupe, Greater Monterrey, Mexico, aerial view of the metal-wrapped, ribbed and undulating shell of the stadium.

184   BBVA Bancomer Stadium, detail of the exterior skin.

BBVA Bancomer Stadium

A second project in Mexico, the BBVA Bancomer Stadium in Greater Monterrey (Populous, 2015), brought a sculptural stadium clad in steel and aluminium to this cosmopolitan city. Monumental concrete structural elements in the circulation spaces highlight the heft and weight of the project, while the vertical metal fins that wrap the facade, narrowing and widening in order to accommodate the undulating roofline, give the project an unmistakably contemporary identity. Inside, the aperture of the roof frames a view of the nearby mountains.

Noto-Lucchesi Stadium

Of course, the places where we might expect to find grand stadia were not dormant in this time period, and there are two projects in France that merit some consideration here. The first, in Marseille, is the Noto-Lucchesi Stadium by Studio NAOM, completed in 2016. The Marseille project, located in a former brownfield site, deploys Cor-Ten steel and green space to revitalise an urban neighbourhood widely regarded as in decline. Faced with this challenging brief, Studio NAOM came up with a playful response that mixes artistic ambitions with grittier urban realities. The result is a landscape that mixes rust and hard edges with green and soft hills, the whole thing looking like nothing else one has seen anywhere before.

186   Noto-Lucchesi Stadium, showing the Cor-Ten steel that is the primary material used throughout.

185   Noto-Lucchesi Stadium, Marseille, France, a multi-purpose urban project with a pitch, a running track, several courts, locker rooms and housing for an on-site manager.

187   Neto-Lucchesi Stadium, showing the
steel fencing that rings the stadium.

188　Noto-Lucchesi Stadium, locker rooms and other functions are tucked into steel pods set into low green mounds.

189　Noto-Lucchesi Stadium, night-time view, highlighting the urban character of the site.

190   Noto-Lucchesi Stadium, conceptual sketch.

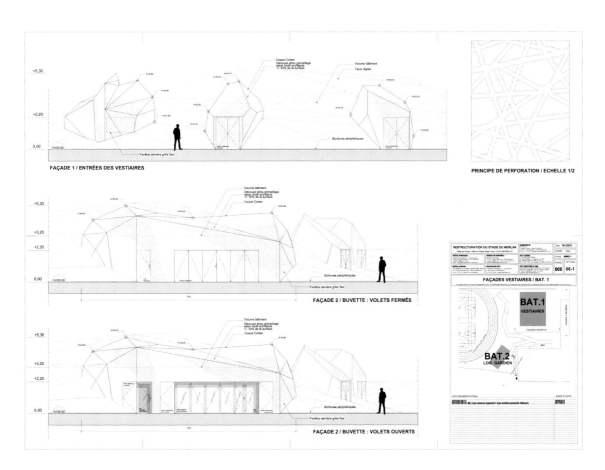

191   Noto-Lucchesi Stadium, drawings illustrating the various facade choices.

192   Leo Lagrange Stadium, Toulon, France, with the sail-like canopy that defines it.

Leo Lagrange Stadium

Another modestly scaled but nevertheless inventive and thoughtful project is the Leo Lagrange Stadium in Toulon (archi5 and Borja Huidobro, 2013). The designers maximised the impact of the site, which sits between the mountains to the north and the Mediterranean Sea, generating a new place-making building for the port area of the city. The stadium is named after the socialist former French Under Secretary of State for Sports, who was in office in the late 1930s as a member of the Popular Front alliance. Lagrange was an advocate of sharing sport across class boundaries as an anti-fascist and anti-militarist practice, so this particular ground has a hefty programme to address and it does so elegantly. A white, sail-like canopy shelters the single stand for 3,500 and a public footbridge brings the public into the ground. The textile roof covers 2,500 square metres and touches the ground at just six points, with generous asymmetrical curves that flow over the seating. Illuminated at night, the fabric roof glows, highlighting the centrality of this public sport venue to the life of the city.

193　Leo Lagrange Stadium, the view from the curving footpath that brings spectators and visitors into the stadium.

194　Leo Lagrange Stadium in its city context, set between the port and the mountains.

(*top left*) 195   Leo Lagrange Stadium illuminated at night.

(*bottom left*) 196   Leo Lagrange Stadium is in dialogue
with both the cityscape and the mountains nearby.

197   Leo Lagrange Stadium, detail of the roof structure.

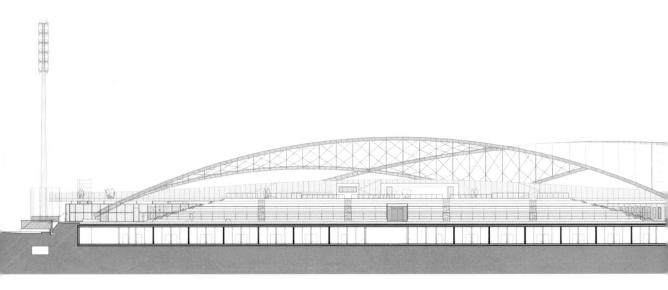

198   Leo Lagrange Stadium, elevation.

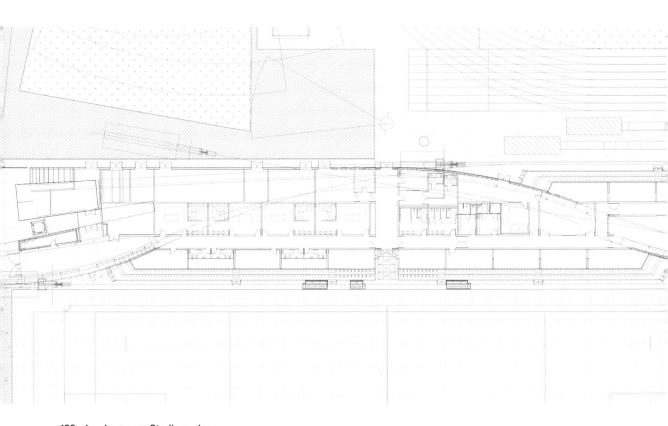

199   Leo Lagrange Stadium, plan.

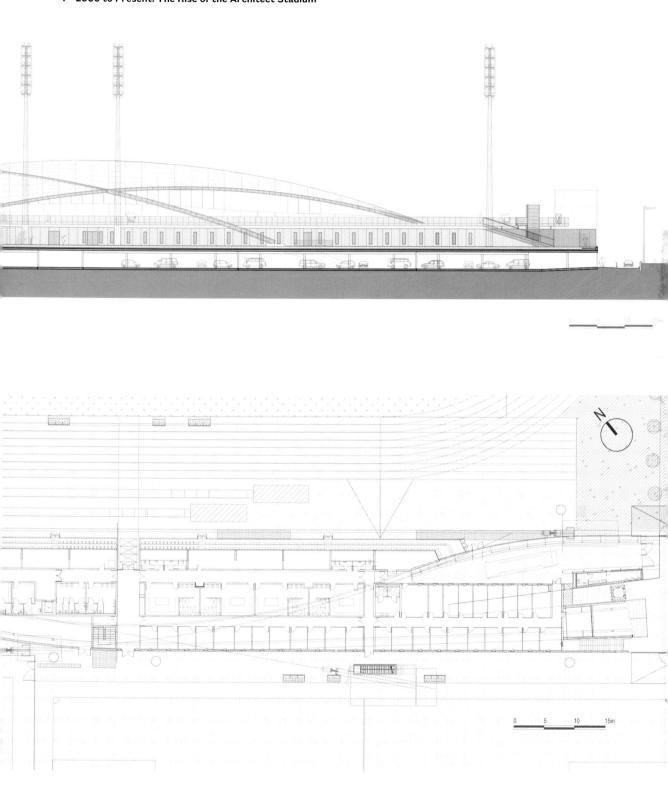

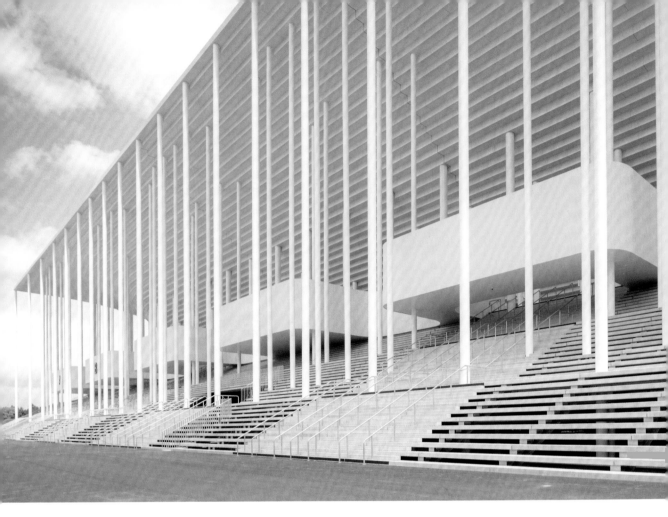

200   New Bordeaux Stadium, France, a pristine white rectangle on an earthen plinth, with a roof resting on a sea of slender columns.

New Bordeaux or Matmut Atlantique Stadium

A Herzog and de Meuron project, variously referred to as the New Bordeaux Stadium or the Matmut Atlantique Stadium, is on the opposite end of the stadium spectrum that we have explored in this chapter. Monumental, relentlessly columned and on the exterior at least ruthlessly trabeated, this all-white rectangle of very carefully designed sporting space is clearly refined, expensive and a very form-conscious backdrop for the games played within.

201   New Bordeaux Stadium, detail of the exterior stairs and columns.

5 Stadia of the Future

Skyscrapers, for most of the first century of their existence, generally were understood as spaces for white-collar labour above all else (to such an extent that we often forgot precisely how much blue-collar labour was required to maintain and operate these structures). It was not until the late 1960s, with projects like the John Hancock Center in Chicago (Skidmore, Owings and Merrill, 1970), that this line of thinking about the building type began to change. Over the next several decades, clients and designers alike embraced the possibility that housing, commercial, entertainment and leisure programmes could now be profitably placed in skyscrapers and complement office space. In many ways, the global ubiquity of the tall building depended on the move away from programmatic rigour and towards programmatic heterogeneity. Today the revolution has come back to the place of the skyscraper's birth, with most new tall buildings in New York City providing housing rather than office space.[31]

Not too long ago I was in discussion with a lead engineer on a $1 billion+ stadium in the United States. I mentioned to her that I thought stadia were the new skyscrapers – that is to say, a building type that for much of its history had been understood as a single-use, often relentlessly pragmatic structure, but one that now was undergoing a renaissance in thinking. She agreed, noting that even among the engineering firms (which are not always tasked with questions about programme) there was a renewed emphasis on thinking about new ways of using and deploying stadium spaces. At the same time, a number of stadium design firms are suggesting that the world (or rather the wealthy bit of it building ever more expensive projects) has reached a state of what I call 'peak stadia'.

The significance of this development (and it is not a certainty that we have reached the 'peak' just yet) could be far-reaching. For instance, the proposed new stadium for Los Angeles, currently called Los Angeles Stadium at Hollywood Park (but likely to change once naming rights are sold) is set to open in 2020. Designed by HKS, it will be home to two National Football League teams in a city famous for not much caring about football and is already estimated to cost $2.6 billion. Actual construction costs will surely be higher. Currently the most expensive building in Los Angeles is the 73-storey Wilshere Grand Center (AC Martins Partners, 2017), which houses office space, a hotel, a shopping mall and restaurants. The tallest building in the USA west of the Mississippi River, it cost $1.2 billion to build. That is well less than half of what the new stadium will cost. Even with two teams, the building will host only 16 home games per year, whereas the Wilshere Grand Center is open for business seven days a week, 365 days a year. So, how does one justify the monumental increase in cost and complexity for a building that hosts so much less actual lived experience? Stadium backers in Los Angeles, like most cities in the USA, claim that the project will anchor significant urban renewal and economic activity. These projections, made before in many other cities, are almost always exaggerated, but persist nevertheless.

The wood revival

New Lawn

If this is peak stadia, then surely the next generation of projects will have to reign costs in while also finding ways to animate the stadium with a greater frequency of activity throughout the lifecycle of the building, rather than on game or concert days alone. Precisely what the post-peak cost to benefit ratio will be is as yet unclear, but there are also other dimensions that might drive innovation going forward. Many of these are emerging first in smaller-scale projects, but they hopefully point towards trends that could take hold over the next decade. The first of these concerns materiality. The lead here is being taken not by a big-money club in a glitzy urban centre, but by a small club in a town of 7,500 people in the south-west of England. There, in Nailsworth, Forest Green Rovers are proposing to build a Zaha Hadid-designed stadium for 5,000 spectators entirely of wood.

202   New Lawn, a rendering of the proposed, nearly all-timber stadium in Nailsworth, Gloucestershire, UK.

203 New Lawn, the tunnel between the dressing rooms and pitch, defined by curved timber members.

Wood, long banished from large public structures due to obvious fire-safety concerns, is re-emerging in large-scale architectural projects. The development of engineered lumber, particularly cross-laminated timber and laminated veneer lumber, and a refreshed understanding of how wood can be a renewable construction material (in a world where construction is the leading driver of energy consumption) all play a role in this project. That several decades have passed, in most industrialised nations at least, since the last of the great stadium fires – Bradford City in 1985 – is also part of the story. The low carbon footprint of wood was a driver in selecting it as the primary building material for the ground that will serve as the anchor tenant for a larger development called Eco Park.

The convergence of a client determined to break out of the standard mould for a stadium, the rise of new timber technologies and the work of a firm with an established tolerance for experimental design has culminated in a novel project that could serve as a model for a whole range of wooden stadia projects in the future. The New Lawn, as the project is called, is designed to allow it to expand to 10,000 seats to accommodate a growing fan base. Aside from the optimism this suggests about the team's future success, it means that nearly all-wood stadia could become options for a wide range of clubs operating in the second and third tiers of sporting leagues around the world.

204 New Lawn, the view at dusk of the
tensile fabric roof.

205 New Lawn and the footbridge to the adjacent business development planned as the economic counterpart to the project.

206 New Lawn on game day.

207   New National Stadium, Japan: Kengo Kuma's proposed Tokyo 2020 Olympic Games stadium,
with a roof structure of Japanese larch wood.

New National Stadium

The resurgence of wood as a building material is not limited, however, to smaller venues alone; it is also returning to monumental urban stadia projects. Most notable in this category is Kengo Kuma's New National Stadium in Tokyo for the 2020 Summer Olympic Games. Seating 80,000, the canopy of the stadium is projected to be a lattice of native-grown larch wood and steel, reflecting the territory of the project in materiality as well as in formal design gestures suggestive of Buddhist pagodas. Other notable design features include plantings located throughout the eaves of the ground and efforts to minimise heating and cooling costs. At the urban scale, the three-tiered stadium is designed to settle into the surrounding green space in a surprisingly unobtrusive fashion for a project of this scale. Many of Kuma's best-known projects depend on a powerful use of concrete. But with this project Kuma has spoken of his interest in 'going beyond the era of concrete', and in using the New National Stadium

208   New National Stadium, interior view.

as a way to resurrect interest in timber construction in a country with a rich heritage of the form and an abundance of cedar and larch. As Kuma said, 'We will show the model of a mature society in the stadium . . . That's the way to live a happy life relying on limited natural resources from a small land.'[32]

209   Kinetic Stadium, Studio Gang's proposal for a stadium set atop a tall building
in Chicago, with stands anchored to nearby buildings.

Finding space for stadia

Ecological critiques of stadia often focus on
the energy consumption, carbon footprint of
construction and economic costs that render the
buildings unsustainable. Another aspect that critics
observe might make 'peak stadia' unsustainable
is the diminishing amount of territory in dense
urban locales in which to locate these monumental
projects. Just as Zaha Hadid Architects have
developed a novel approach on materiality, another
firm – Studio Gang – is looking at novel solutions to
the problem of siting relative to urban stadia.

Kinetic Stadium, as the project is known,
imagines how Chicago might accommodate a
new baseball park in the heart of the downtown
district. This is of course some of the most
sought-after and densely occupied real estate in
the city. Finding a multi-acre site available for new
construction is not an option. Nor is demolition
of existing structures to clear a large enough site
economically feasible. So, what to do? Studio
Gang looked at the district and saw a space that
others had missed – on top of the skyscrapers that

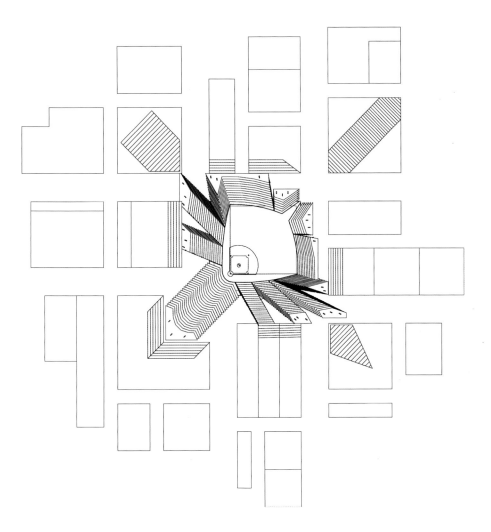

210   Kinetic Stadium, site plan.

fill downtown. So, the firm proposed a structure that would, in their words, 'employ a kinetic seating bowl, lifted 30 floors above street level, comprised of a series of transforming seating and support elements, many constructed to fold into the adjacent high-rise buildings in a dense urban center'.[33]

The innovation of this project is to delink the stadium from the ground plane from which it first emerged nearly 3,000 years ago. The modern-day stand, after all, was originally a hillside or slope where spectators sat – the ground has always been key to the stadium. The shift here, situating a monumental project atop another one, is surreal at first glance, but then again, so are skyscrapers in many ways. Whether this proposal will ever be realised is impossible to know, but without doubt it has propelled the discussion around the future of the building type in a new direction.

211   Kinetic Stadium, rendering of how this sport architecture fantasy might play out.

Environmental and economic sustainability

Temporary structures

The quest to address sustainability compelled both the International Olympic Committee and the Fédération Internationale de Football Association to issue their own standards for sustainability in stadium construction.[34] The first result of those calls in many ways was the bid by the city of Boston in the United States for the 2020 Summer Games. The centrepiece of that bid was a disappearing stadium: a project that would hold 60,000 people but would be temporary, designed to be dismantled after the Games. The great challenge of the Olympics historically is the question of legacy use of the stadium and buildings constructed to host the range of athletic events. In particularly egregious cases – Athens in 2004 and Rio de Janeiro in 2016 – the legacy planning was essentially non-existent and those cities were left saddled with monumental liabilities related to those venues.[35] So Boston's innovation was to remove the question of legacy from the obligations around the single largest venue for the Games – the Olympic Stadium.

The stadium in the Boston scenario would be 'temporary', a quality that is somewhat easier to envision in a ground holding 1,000 or 2,000 spectators. A four- to five-storey structure with accommodations for the safety, comfort and security of 60,000 spectators, hundreds of athletes and the media scrum that goes along with all of that is much more challenging to imagine fully realised. Indeed, it may be that what Boston was really proposing was not a novel design that was lightweight, modular and demountable in the way most designers would imagine a 'temporary' structure, but rather a fully realised $1 billion dollar project that after the Games would simply be demolished. That this truly 'surreal' proposal is actually sustainable is hard to believe, but it may represent a line of thinking that clients and cities are more willing to adopt than the more idiosyncratic proposals such as the Kinetic Stadium or a nearly all-wood stadium.[36]

Modular construction

In this mode, Populous announced in 2017 that they were designing a modular football stadium in San Diego, USA, for a second division football team, 1904 FC. The firm describes the design strategy as 'permanent modular construction', where pods assembled off-site are slotted into the site-built grandstands. Designed for a capacity of 10,000 spectators, the permanent modular construction method has the advantage of reducing construction time and in turn construction costs, which for this project are a very modest $15 million. In spite of the low budget, the design team and clients for the San Diego project have made it clear that they are looking for a stadium that will build team identity and offer a memorable game-day experience. These are aspirations for smaller grounds that in previous decades were secondary to more pragmatic concerns, suggesting that one of the potential benefits of modularity is its potential to advance the more ephemeral and qualitative aspects of the stadium experience.

The proposal for 1904 FC followed on the heels of the news that one of the stadia for the 2022 World Cup in Qatar would also be modular and incorporate recycled shipping containers. Modularity has for decades been proffered as a way of addressing ecological and economic concerns about stadia and their legacy costs. But it has never been designed and delivered at scale – that is to say, realised at the same seating capacity as conventional, 'permanent' stadia. The Populous project is a modest improvement in terms of scale, but the proposed stadium for Qatar, seating 40,000, if realised would represent a dramatic step forward in the integration of modular construction in this building type. There is some question, however, whether what is realisable in Qatar can serve as a model for other places. A small, oil-rich nation ruled by a monarchy is hardly an analogous environment to much of the rest of the world where stadia are built. How and in what fashion the advances made with Doha's modular stadium can be translated to cities elsewhere remains to be seen.

Modularity at present is mostly deployed as a means of reducing the cost and carbon footprint of stadia rather than as a driver of formal, aesthetic ambitions. There are, nevertheless, many possibilities afforded by modular construction that could generate a range of formal opportunities well worth exploring. At a minimum, modularity suggests the possibility of a flexible facade that would allow the public appearance of the stadium to change over time and in response to internal and external events. Flexible facade strategies would also make it easier for a single stadium to host more than one club, a longstanding challenge in many cities where two clubs share a ground. Currently variations in lighting schemes have been the main way to address expressions of club identity in stadia with two clubs – the Allianz Arena turned from red to blue when 1860 München played rather than Bayern for instance. But with a modular facade, significantly more robust variation could take place. The same would be true for using the stadium for non-sporting events. Pushed to its logical extremes, modularity could even allow for a greater embrace of the spatial possibilities of a multi-use stadium, one that operated seven days a week on a year-round basis.

Visions for the future

Other visions of the future of the stadium are focused on how changes in the form of the building type might evolve in the future, reinventing what we know about the physical experience of being in the ground. Stadia, football stadia in particular, are distinct among building types in that they explicitly focus our attention on the ground – the field or pitch – where the game is played. Given the long history of the type, this is not surprising. After all, the circus and the stadion – the precedents from classical antiquity for the modern stadium – were often carved from the earth itself rather than built to sit upon it. Indeed, such is the connection between the two elements that stadia are routinely called 'grounds'. One recent proposition offers a tantalising look at how the future of this building

type might radically exploit the tension between building and ground. Sited in the desert of the city of Al Ain in Abu Dhabi, the aptly named Rock Stadium by MZ Architects proposes to burrow both stand and ground into the surrounding arid landscape. Here the stadium no longer offers a heroic elevation to approaching spectators (although precisely who would attend or use this ground remains unclear at present). Instead, a typology broadly associated with a towering mass enclosing the field of play is turned, well, neither inside out nor upside down, but something of both. This applies not only to the form of the stadium, but to its programme as well, as there is no proper demand for such a building; nor is the climate, even when buried into the ground, suitable for outdoor sporting events for most of the year. Nor is there robust attendance at existing venues in the country, with crowds for football matches averaging less than 4,000.

On the outskirts of Paris, SCAU Architects, whose work on the Stade Velodrome we saw earlier, are proposing a 'vegetated stadium'. The stadium, which is due to be completed in time for the 2024 Summer Olympic Games in Paris, is located on the edge of a forest, and the design calls for not just a green roof, but also planted walls, with the stands tucked into the natural slope of the site. A system of skylights, light channels and mirrors will channel light down into the stadium during the day. At night, in theory, with the ground illuminated from within, the effect will be reversed.

Security developments

Discussions about the future of the stadium will inevitably also involve thorny problems from other parts of public life. One of those that is already coming to the fore is a debate about the role of technology in securing stadia. A range of novel responses geared towards addressing security concerns of stadia owners and operators is already being developed and marketed at an increasing pace, particularly in the area of face-scanning technology. There are legitimate concerns about public safety at stadia in a post 9/11 world where terrorist groups increasingly target civilians. The 2015 attack on the Stade de France, part of the larger attacks on Paris in November of that year, highlighted that in the future stadia are likely to be targeted again. Standard crowd security measures such as metal detectors, bag searches and physical pat-downs are very time-consuming and often generate lengthy queues. These, of course, present a challenge to the ingress of paying spectators and a threat to the fan experience that draws them to the venue and away from their televisions.

Firms have been quick to market technological intermediaries to address this concern, among them face-recognition technology. These systems depend on scanning the face of every spectator who enters the stadium and raise considerable concerns about privacy in the public sphere. Early adopters of this technology in the USA have used it to manage and track employees at arenas and stadia (with their agreement) but enterprise-scale deployment would demand that all visitors to the stadium be scanned. What happens to those images once the match is over? How will cases of mistaken identity be adjudicated? Does one have the right to anonymity in a stadium? This is an especially critical question. In 2017, at the Champions League Final at the Millennium Stadium in Wales (Bligh Lobb Sports Architecture, 1999), police deployed facial recognition technology to scan 170,000 people. Of those, 2,470 were identified as criminals. The technology, in fact, was not just slightly wrong, but massively so: it had a 92 per cent false positive rate.[37] Thousands of innocent persons attending the match between Real Madrid and Juventus were tagged as criminals, without their knowledge. How does one seek redress from such surveillance, when communication of its presence is unavailable to the public?

In the United States, the largest concert ticket vendor in the country recently announced that it was forming a partnership with a facial recognition technology company in order to trial the use of identity technologies in lieu of a physical ticket.[38] At present technology is fast outstripping policy on these matters.

The stadium as an index of change

Developments around technology and materiality related to stadia are often about return on investment. And stadia, even small ones, are projects that involve major financial outlay. In the United States the bulk of reporting about stadia takes place in the business section of the newspaper rather than the sports pages. The history of stadia makes it clear that this is a reductive vision, as the previous chapters demonstrate. The future of the stadium is about more than technology, or modularity, or advances in materials and building methods. As monumental, largely urban places of public congregation, stadia can be an index of change in society. This is a topic that could occupy a volume of its own, but some examples of this are worth touching on with respect to the future of the building type. In 2018 Saudi Arabian authorities announced that for the first time in the nation's history women would be allowed to attend football matches. They would, of course, be restricted to women-only sections in the grounds, and only allowed in three stadia, at least initially.[39] The decision to allow women into stadia was widely interpreted as a marker of a larger movement to loosen the grip of conservative leaders over public life in the kingdom.

Accessibility in stadia, for at least the past three decades, has been seen as a measure of equity. Inclusion of spaces that could accommodate more than working-class men was a first step. Changes that embraced attendance by families were another. Regulations requiring accessibility for those in wheelchairs or with other mobility constraints were another still. These have all been indicators of progress. But it is also the case that stadium regulations can be indicators of stubborn obstacles to change. This continues to be the case in Iran, where women are still forbidden to attend almost all public sporting events. In 2018, women who wish to watch a football match must dress up as men, and risk arrest if they are caught. In both Iran and Saudi Arabia, an autocratic regime understands that the regulation of access to a stadium is about far more than attendance at a game. The symbolic heft of the stadium remains in place across the political spectrum.

The ideology of stadia

In some ways the debates about the future of the stadium – and whether it will indeed be transformed in the coming years as dramatically as the skyscraper has – take us back to a debate that occupied the world of architecture for the two decades following World War II. In the wake of the deployment of monumental architecture by the fascist regimes of Germany and Italy, and with the rise of state-mandated Socialist Realism in the Soviet Union, architects in Western Europe and the United States had to grapple with what sort of monumental architecture could stand in for the values of capitalist democracy and an ostensibly liberated, pluralist Western society going forward. There were debates in cities around the world about precisely what types of programmes could properly be monumental in scale, and under what aesthetic conditions monumental architecture could be freed from association with tyrannical rule by either the left or the right.

This was a particularly critical issue as the end of World War II saw the return of wide-scale urban construction after more than two decades of economic depression and the subsequent privations of the war. Today the debates about monumentality are less overtly cast in ideological terms (although they are in truth heavily freighted with ideological matters), and more often assessed along objective lines of economic return and ecological cost. This is, on the one hand, appropriate. But it is not the only measure we should be taking into account when considering these projects. As neo-liberal central governments across the United Kingdom, Europe and North America reign in investments in urban redevelopment (and in the case of the USA, this has been the case now for at least four decades), it is left to a host of private actors to fill the void. Around the world stadia are the projects that cities turn to when attempting to regenerate

neighbourhoods and commercial districts. Urban monumental architecture today is more often than not at least in part yoked to stadia construction.

This is true across geographies, in large and small countries, in rich and less rich cities, and in both politically conservative and ostensibly progressive places alike. The use of public funds in the American context immediately makes these stadia projects 'political' in nature. It is also true, of course, that even when these projects do not have public funds attached to them, they nevertheless demand urban territory that is part of the public sphere, and so even then they are 'political' projects. What is so notable about the stadium in the twenty-first century is that, even with all of the knowledge we have about the possibilities and limits of the building type, even with all that we know about what economic impact it can (and more likely can't) have, and even though we are all clear that the vast majority of stadia are public subsidies for private, revenue-generating enterprises, we still continue to build them at an impressive rate. Indeed, even countries that in the past largely avoided the political misjudgement of using public funds for stadia are now falling prey to this habit. In the UK, as this book went to press, the English Football Association announced tentative plans to sell New Wembley to Shahid Khan, the American owner of the NFL Jacksonville Jaguars and London's own Fulham FC, for £600 billion. This is well less than it cost to build a decade ago, after ten years of massive increases in property values in the capital. All of this is a reminder that a stadium, in the end, is not an asset but a liability. It is also a pointed reminder that not only are sporting clubs increasingly commodities owned by a narrow band of transnational global billionaires, but so too are stadia, even those that are regarded as the 'crown jewel' of a nation. This ownership is not risk-free, as the Football Association learned when the financing costs of New Wembley drained the coffers of the organisation, preventing them from investing in growing the domestic game. The same is true for clubs, who sometimes find their stadium ambition greater than their reserve of assets, such as in the New Spurs Stadium, where the initial cost estimates have gone from £400 million to now threatening to reach £1 billion. The yearly interest charges on that amount will deprive the club of funds to pay for new players, even with the revenue growth that the 62,000-seat stadium (and its higher ticket prices) will generate.

One way to assess the priorities of a given society is to study the distribution of funds and the allocation of territory. In this case the vast amount of money and land ceded to stadia, whether in 'progressive' Los Angeles or 'conservative' Las Vegas, wealthy, cosmopolitan London or gritty Liverpool, or myriad other cities around the world, is certainly telling and often problematic.

The future of the stadium will inevitably have to grapple with this reality more successfully than it has in the past. The future of the stadium, then, is not just a question of design, or of technological innovation. It is also about a reckoning that will have to be made about the historical forces and political choices made over the past three decades that led us to this moment. What virtues will we decide to reward with territory and cash in the future? Which onerous costs and side-effects will we determine are no longer tolerable? And how will we design the forms that the proper answers to such questions will require? This is the central debate for the future of the stadium.

Notes

1.   Arsene Wenger, quoted in Andrew Anthony, 'Arsene Wenger: The Blinkered Visionary', *Observer Profile, The Guardian* (3 September 2011).

2.   For one of the more famous accounts of being an Arsenal supporter in the 1970s and 1980s, see Nick Hornby, *Fever Pitch* (London: Riverhead Books, 1998).

3.   The transformation of Arsenal under Arsene Wenger is itself a topic covered in a number of books, including: Alex Flynn and Kevin Whitcher, *Arsenal: The Making of a Modern Superclub* (Kingston, England: Vision Sports Publishing, 2016); Amy Lawrence and Stuart MacFarlane, *The Wenger Revolution: Twenty Years of Arsenal* (London: Bloomsbury Sport, 2016); and John Cross, *Arsene Wenger: The Inside Story of Arsenal Under Wenger* (New York: Simon and Schuster, 2016).

4.   For a more detailed exploration of this issue, see Benjamin Flowers, *Sport and Architecture* (London: Routledge, 2017).

5.   Neville Gabie, *Posts* (London: Penguin, 1999), p.i.

6.   For a comprehensive history of the Astrodome and stadia in the United States generally during the postwar era, see Benjamin D. Lisle, *Modern Coliseum: Stadiums and American Culture* (Philadelphia: University of Pennsylvania Press, 2017).

7.   For a comprehensive survey of Olympic projects, see Geraint John and Dave Parker, *Olympic Stadia: Their History, Their Design, Their Future* (London: Routledge, 2019).

8.   Richard Crawford, 'Floating Stadium on Mission Bay Really Couldn't Hold Water', *San Diego Union-Tribune* (2 September 2010).

9.   For a discussion of other stadia with unusual relationships to their site, see Benjamin Flowers, 'Sporting Grounds', *Offramp 11: GROUND* (http://sciarc-offramp.info/ground/sporting-grounds).

10.   A particularly strong discussion of this trend, focusing on France, can be found in Robert W. Lewis, *The Stadium Century: Sport, Spectatorship and Mass Society in Modern France* (Manchester: Manchester University Press, 2017).

11.   For a history of the economic and political forces shaping stadia, see Robert Trumpbour, *The New Cathedrals: Politics and Media in the History of Stadium Construction* (Syracuse: Syracuse University Press, 2007).

12.   Alan Travis, 'Thatcher Government Toyed with Evacuating Liverpool after 1981 Riots', *The Guardian* (29 December 2011).

13.   Steven A. Reiss, 'Historical Perspectives on Sports and Public Policy', in Wilbur C. Roth, ed., *The Economics and Politics of Sports Facilities* (Westport, CT: Quorum Books, 2000), p.29.

14.   Roger Agnell, quoted in Lisle, *Modern Coliseum*, p.229.

15.   ibid., p.234.

16.   Joseph Malinconico, 'Roosevelt Stadium: Glory Fading Fast', *New York Times* (28 November 1982).

17.   'West Ham: London Stadium Should be Knocked Down, Says Expert', *BBC Sport* (31 October 2016, retrieved 9 December 2016).

18.   Archibald Leitch, despite being one of the most prolific stadium architects in the world, largely fell out of most histories of sport and sporting architecture. That oversight has begun to be corrected by Simon Inglis in *Engineering Archie: Archibald Leitch – Football Ground Designer* (London: English Heritage, 2005); see also Simon Inglis, 'Meet Archibald Leitch: The Man Who Invented the Modern Football Stadium', *FourFourTwo* (November 2015).

19.   For a more comprehensive study of the fire and the subsequent investigation, see Martin Fletcher, *Fifty-Six: The Story of the Bradford Fire* (London: Bloomsbury Sport, 2015).

20.   For more on Hillsborough and its aftermath, see Phil Scraton, *Hillsborough – The Truth* (Edinburgh: Mainstream Publishing, 2016); and Adrian Tempany, *And the Sun Shines Now: How Hillsborough and the Premier League Changed Britain* (London: Faber and Faber, 2016).

21. Geraint John, Rod Sheard and Ben Vickery, *Stadia: The Populous Design and Development Guide*, 5th edn (New York: Routledge, 2013).

22. This process is fraught with complications across a number of political and economic fronts, an issue explored in some depth by Mark Panton and Geoff Walters in '"It's Just a Trojan Horse for Gentrification": Austerity and Stadium-led Regeneration', *International Journal of Sports Policy and Politics*, vol.10, no.1 (2018), pp.163–83.

23. Robert Hughes, speaking in 'Mies van der Rohe – Less is More', episode 2 of the 2003 BBC documentary series *Visions of Space*.

24. Jeffrey Kipnis, 'When the Big Red Team Takes the Field', in Todd Gannon, *Eisenman Architects Home Field Advantage: University of Phoenix Stadium* (New York: Princeton Architectural Press, 2008), p.154.

25. The redevelopment in East London associated with the Olympics has been a subject of debate and controversy. For a more detailed assessment, see Phil Cohen and Paul Watt, eds, *London 2012 and the Post-Olympics City: A Hollow Legacy?* (London: Palgrave Macmillan, 2017).

26. IDOM Architects, *New Pasaron Stadium* (June 2012), press release.

27. IDOM Architects, *San Mamés: New Stadium* (August 2014), press release. www.bilbaostadium.com.

28. Rudy Ricciotti, 'Stade Jean Bouin', in www.formakers.eu (22 December 2013), accessed 5 June 2018.

29. Populous, *Soccer City Stadium* (July 2015), press release.

30. See David Goldblatt and Daniel Nolan, 'Viktor Orban's Reckless Football Obsession', *The Guardian* (11 January 2018).

31. For a more detailed look at the history of the postwar skyscraper, see Benjamin Flowers, *Skyscraper: The Politics and Power of Building New York City in the Twentieth Century* (Philadelphia: University of Pennsylvania Press, 2009).

32. Kengo Kuma, quoted in 'Olympic Stadium Architect Sees Wood as a Way to Change Tokyo's Concrete Legacy', *The Japan Times* (30 May 2017).

33. Studio Gang, *Architectural Record, Transcending Type* (July 2004), press release.

34. The IOC proposals for future sustainability of the Olympic Games came in the report *Olympic Agenda 2020: 20+20 Recommendations* (Lausanne, Switzerland: International Olympic Committee, 2014). FIFA now issues a 'sustainability report' for each World Cup detailing efforts put in place to enhance recycling, reduce energy consumption and so on at the competition.

35. See Judith Grant Long, *Olympic Urbanism: Rome to Rio* (London: Routledge, 2017).

36. On the impact that rising construction and security costs are having on the nature of which cities are likely to bid on the Olympic Games in the future, see Chris Dempsey and Andrew Zimbalist, *No Boston Olympics: How and Why Smart Cities are Passing on the Torch* (Lebanon, New Hampshire: University of New Hampshire Press, 2017).

37. Press Association, 'Welsh Police Wrongly Identify Thousands as Potential Criminals', *The Guardian* (5 May 2018).

38. Anne Steele, 'Ticketmaster's New Challenge: Your Face', *Wall Street Journal* (4 May 2018).

39. Kareem Shaheen, 'Saudi Football Stadium Welcomes Women for First Time', *The Guardian* (12 January 2018).

Further Reading

Agnew, Paddy, *Forza Italia: A Journey in Search of Italy and its Football* (London: Ebury Press, 2006).

Alegi, Peter, *Laduma! Soccer, Politics, and Society in South Africa* (Scottsville: University of KwaZulu-Natal Press, 2004).

Bale, John, *Sport, Space and the City* (London: Routledge, 1993).

Bale, John, *Landscapes of Modern Sport* (New York: St. Martin's Press, 1994).

Clarke, Stuart, *The Homes of Football* (Liverpool: Bluecoat Press, 2013).

Culley, Peter, and Pasco, John, *Sports Facilities and Technologies* (London: Routledge, 2009).

Danish Institute for Sports Studies, *World Stadium Index: Stadiums Built for Major Sporting Events – Bright Future or Future Burden?* (Copenhagen: DISS, 2012).

Delaney, Kevin J., and Eckstein, Rick, *Public Dollars, Private Stadiums: The Battle Over Building Sports Stadiums* (New Brunswick, NJ: Rutgers University Press, 2003).

Flowers, Benjamin, 'Stadiums: Architecture and Iconography of the Beautiful Game', *International Journal of the History of Sport*, vol.28, nos 8–9 (2011), pp.1174–85.

Flowers, Benjamin, *Sport and Architecture* (London: Routledge, 2017).

Frank, Sybille, and Steets, Silke, *Stadium Worlds: Football, Space, and the Built Environment* (London: Routledge, 2010).

Gabie, Neville, *Posts* (London: Penguin, 1999).

Gaffney, Christopher, *Temples of the Earthbound Gods: Stadiums in the Cultural Landscapes of Rio de Janeiro and Buenos Aires* (Austin: University of Texas Press, 2008).

Galeano, Eduardo, *Football in Sun and Shadow* (London: Verso, 2003).

Goldblatt, David, *The Ball is Round: A Global History of Football* (New York: Viking, 2006).

Horne, John, and Whannel, Garry, *Understanding the Olympics* (London: Routledge, 2016).

Huggins, Mike, and O'Mahoney, Mike, eds, *The Visual in Sport* (London: Routledge, 2011).

Inglis, Simon, *The Football Grounds of Great Britain* (London: Willow, 1987).

Inglis, Simon, *The Football Grounds of Europe* (London: Willow, 1990).

Inglis, Simon, *Engineering Archie: Archibald Leitch – Football Ground Designer* (London: English Heritage, 2005).

John, Geraint, and Parker, Dave, *Olympic Stadia: Their History, Their Design, Their Future* (London: Routledge, 2019).

John, Geraint, Sheard, Rod, and Vickery, Ben, *Stadia: The Populous Design and Development Guide*, 5th edn (New York: Routledge, 2013).

Kierkuc-Bielinski, Jerry, and John, Geraint, *Stadia: Sport and Vision in Architecture*, Soane Gallery exhibition catalogue (London: Soane Gallery, 2012).

Lewis, Robert W., *The Stadium Century: Sport, Spectatorship and Mass Society in Modern France* (Manchester: Manchester University Press, 2017).

Lisle, Benjamin D., *Modern Coliseum: Stadiums and American Culture* (Philadelphia: University of Pennsylvania Press, 2017).

Long, Judith Grant, *Olympic Urbanism: Rome to Rio* (London: Routledge, 2017).

Nixdorf, Stefan, *Stadium Atlas: Technical Recommendations for Grandstands in Modern Stadia* (Berlin: Ernst & Sohn, 2008).

Provoost, Michelle, ed., *The Stadium: The Architecture of Mass Sport* (Rotterdam: Nederlands Architectuurinstituut, 2000).

Trumpbour, Robert, *The New Cathedrals: Politics and Media in the History of Stadium Construction* (Syracuse: Syracuse University Press, 2007).

Wells, Cassandra, *Football Grounds from the Air* (London: Myriad Books, 2006).

Wimmer, Martin, *Construction and Design Manual: Stadium Buildings* (Berlin: DOM Publishers, 2016).

Zimbalist, Andrew, *Circus Maximus: The Economic Gamble Behind Hosting the Olympics and the World Cup* (Washington, DC: Brookings Institution Press, 2015).

Index

Note: *italic* page numbers indicate illustrations; numbers in brackets preceded by *n* are endnote numbers.

Illustration Credits

Reproduction of all illustrations listed below (by figure number) is courtesy of the following copyright holders: